REST IN PEACE

REST IN PEACE

A PLANNING GUIDE FOR THE INEVITABLE

CHARLES WALTS

AND

TOMMYE WHITE

NEXT CENTURY
PUBLISHING

Rest in Peace
A Planning Guide for the Inevitable

Published by Next Century Publishing
Las Vegas, Nevada
www.NextCenturyPublishing.com

ISBN: 978-1-68102-149-2
Library of Congress Control Number: 2016938344

Printed in the United States of America

PREFACE

Rest in Peace is a pre-death planning guide. It is a manual written to help you plan and prepare for the end of your life or the death of someone for whom you may need to attend to their end-of-life affairs. *Rest in Peace* is also a valuable repository of information about death care services and the things that must be done following the death of a loved one, especially a spouse or significant other.

Two types of people are likely to read and use this manual: those who want (or need) to put their affairs in order before they die, and those who will need the information this manual contains in order to effectively deal with the consequences of a death in the family. Whichever the case, one of the most important documents in this manual is a comprehensive worksheet for collecting vital personal information that will be extremely valuable to survivors of the deceased.

This manual also contains sample templates for important documents such as a will, a durable and medical power of attorney, an advance directive, and an out-of-hospital do-not-resuscitate order. These templates are designed for easy understanding and completion and can serve as valuable tools to help you put your affairs in order before it's too late.

If this planning manual serves no other purpose, it will make you think about all of the things that will happen to you, your possessions, and your loved ones after you have passed on. By following the guidance and directions this manual contains, you can help ensure that your survivors are taken care of and know what to do when you die.

If you have a computer and Internet access, you could certainly find much of the information contained in this manual yourself. But it would require a significant amount of time to do extensive online research from a multitude of sources. To save you the time and effort, we have done the research for you. We have also consulted directly with attorneys, public officials, death care providers, and others to obtain supplemental and clarifying information. As a result, this manual is a compilation of what we believe is the essential information you and your loved ones should have in the event of a death in the family.

If you have any comments or suggestions for the improvement of this manual, please feel free to contact the authors via e-mail at charleswalts2@gmail.com.

FOREWORD

BY
CHARLES WALTS

The inspiration for this planning guide came from Sandy, the widow of a retired Army officer. This manual is dedicated to her.

One morning at a meeting of the breakfast club to which Sandy and I had belonged for more than twenty years, Sandy told me that she was having a difficult time dealing with many of the matters which arose following the death of her husband, Raymond. She said a reference guide would have been very helpful and asked me why no one had ever written a book about who to call and what to do when a family member dies. I didn't have an answer.

For at least six months prior to his death, Raymond had known that he had incurable cancer. Yet in the last months and days of his life, he made no effort to put his affairs in order or prepare Sandy and their adult children to deal with the consequences of his death. When Raymond died, as expected, Sandy and the family were left clueless. They had no idea where vital documents such as a will, insurance policies, property deeds, and military service records were located. Moreover, when Raymond's military retirement pay stopped on the day he died, Sandy was left in financial straits with a lack of ready cash to meet immediate needs and no regular source of income other than Social Security. As a result, in addition to the grief of losing her spouse, Sandy had to deal with a major disruption in her life, having virtually no knowledge of what to do or where to go for assistance.

Thinking about the question Sandy asked that morning at breakfast, I realized that the death of a family member, especially a spouse, is in many ways similar to a major corporate business disruption. Having been a business continuity and disaster recovery consultant to Fortune 500 companies and numerous government agencies and other businesses for more than twenty-five years, I knew that many of the concepts and principles I had learned and used to develop contingency and disaster recovery plans for my clients would also apply to a death in the family.

I contacted my business partner, Tommye White, and asked if she'd consider helping me write a manual about preparing for death. Tommye has as much, if not more experience than I do helping public and private organizations prepare for a major business disruption and avert the potentially disastrous consequences. She agreed to help, and together we began researching and documenting what a person should do to put personal affairs in order before passing on and identifying the issues the family of a recently deceased loved one would have to handle. As a result of our work, this manual was born.

As Tommye and I thought about the target readership for this manual, we initially focused on senior citizens and military retirees. But when we considered the body of work in its entirety, it became readily apparent that most of the information contained herein is applicable to anyone who needs to know who to call and what to do when a family member dies. All that is required for this manual to be a valuable asset is for the reader to face the fact that one day each of us will die and put forth a little effort to plan and prepare for what will happen when death occurs.

We hope this book will help you with the challenges you may face when dealing with the loss of a loved one and that it will also be a help to your loved ones in the event of your death.

ACKNOWLEDGMENTS

Several people provided assistance in the development of this manual. Each one provided essential information without which this manual would not be complete. The authors would like to acknowledge and thank the following individuals for their interest and support in making this book a reality.

Beth H. Smith
Justice of the Peace
Precinct 2, Hays County, Texas

Darrin W. Stanton
Attorney at Law
Dallas, Texas

Bill Pennington
President
Pennington Funeral Home
San Marcos, Texas

Larry Levi
Vice President - Investments
Wells Fargo Advisors

Austin, Texas
Jimmy Lee Stanford
Emergency Management Consultant
Ft. Worth, Texas

Kate Shayler
Website Developer
San Marcos, Texas

Paul C. Velte IV
Attorney and Counselor at Law
San Marcos, Texas

Jude Prather
Hays County Veterans Services Officer
San Marcos, Texas

Charles R. Haynes
Funeral Director
Pennington Funeral Home
San Marcos, Texas

Chas O. Walts
Emergency Management Consultant
Ft. Worth, Texas

Cindy Gallaher
Copy Editor
Arlington, Texas

ABOUT THE AUTHORS

Charles Walts and **Tommye White** are both certified business continuity planners. Between them, Mr. Walts and Ms. White have over sixty years of combined consulting experience developing contingency plans for private sector corporations and government agencies.

Mr. Walts served for more than twenty-six years in the United States Army where he retired at the rank of Colonel in 1988. Subsequent to his retirement from military service, Mr. Walts served for seven years as the information technology strategic and disaster recovery planner for the Texas Education Agency.

In 1997, Mr. Walts became a professional business continuity and disaster recovery consultant for a large BCP/DR consulting firm. Mr. Walts developed more than 300 business and government agency continuity and disaster recovery plans for organizations in the United States, Canada, China, Japan, and Puerto Rico before becoming an independent contingency planning consultant in 2009.

Ms. White has more than thirty-five years of experience in business and government contingency planning. For the past seventeen years, Ms. White has worked as an independent contingency planning consultant where she worked with many companies and developed recovery plans and trained hundreds of companies' employees. From 1986 to 1996, Ms. White was the Manager of Information Technology Administrative Services and Disaster Recovery for the Texas State Comptroller of Public Accounts. During 1996 and 1997 Ms. White worked for a large BCP/DR consulting firm, where she was responsible for providing professional business recovery services.

Ms. White is an experienced national conference speaker and continuing education instructor for business and technology availability planning at the University of Texas and Texas A&M University.

INTRODUCTION

We don't like to think or talk about death. And when we do, it is usually difficult for us. Nonetheless, we are not immortal and dying is inevitable. Sooner or later each and every one of us is going to pass away. The question is, "Will we and our loved ones be ready when that time comes?"

All too often, death comes with little or no warning. But if we are willing to confront our own mortality and plan for the end of our life, we can significantly reduce the stress on our loved ones. By putting our personal affairs in order and providing our survivors with essential information, including our wishes concerning the disposition of our possessions and our desires regarding the handling of our remains, we can greatly lessen the burden on those we leave behind.

The process of putting our affairs in order will take some time and a little effort, but it needs to be done. To delay is to set up a potential hardship for our survivors.

Emotionally, what can be expected when a loved one dies? When a death in the immediate family occurs, it can be one of the most traumatic, sorrowful, and disruptive events ever encountered by the next-of-kin. A surviving spouse may be faced with learning to live alone, and the income that the spouse or family has relied on may come to an abrupt end and create a financial hardship. The surviving family members will be emotionally upset or distraught. Virtually everyone affected by the death of a family member is likely to experience grief as well as a wide range of other emotions.

In 1969, based on her work with cancer patients, psychiatrist Elisabeth Kübler-Ross identified the emotions experienced following a tragedy such as the death of a loved one as the five stages of grief. Ms. Kübler-Ross proposed that the feelings of those who have experienced a death or tragedy will follow a pattern of five emotional response phases in the grieving process.

These response phases include denial, anger, bargaining, depression, and finally, acceptance. The grieving process from denial to acceptance has no particular structure or timeline. Each person grieves in his own way and in his own time. There is no right or wrong way to grieve, and no single way of grieving is better than any other.

For those who find a death difficult to accept and the grief hard to handle, counseling is available from a variety of sources. When a person's grief-related thoughts and behaviors are unusually distressing, individual grief counseling and therapy are effective ways for the bereaved to learn to accept the loss they have sustained.

Beyond the grief, how well will those we leave behind be prepared to deal with the consequences of our death? When we die, will we have done all we can do to prepare our survivors to deal with our passing? For those left behind, especially a spouse, life changes dramatically. A friend and companion is gone, income and cash flow may be affected, and there are a myriad of details to which survivors must attend.

Among the things that will require attention are:

- Making arrangements for the funeral and burial of the deceased;

- Locating critical documents such as the will, birth and marriage certificates, military service records (if applicable), and insurance policies;

- Dealing with financial matters such as insurance claims, bank accounts, and investment accounts;

- Handling property issues;

- Probating the will; and

- Applying for survivor benefits with the Social Security Administration and, if the deceased was a veteran, the Veterans Administration.

If no pre-death plans have been made, the decisions the survivors will have to make may be difficult and stressful, especially if the deceased left no will or instructions regarding his or her property and/or personal desires concerning a funeral and burial or cremation.

By preparing ahead of time (i.e., by doing estate planning, making a will, and pre-planning funeral and burial arrangements), the burden on surviving family members can be greatly diminished.

Regardless of your age, this planning guide is written to help you plan and prepare for your eventual demise. It is also written to prepare your spouse or significant other and your immediate family members to effectively cope with the consequences of your death.

We strongly recommend that you include your spouse and immediate family members in the pre-death planning process.

This planning guide has been developed from two perspectives: a) What can be done before a person's demise to prepare for his or her death, and b) what must be done after death by the decedent's family and/or the designated executor of the deceased's estate. While reading this planning guide will be highly informative, reading it isn't all that's required. This planning guide contains forms and checklists that allow you to collect and record essential personal data prior to your passing. It contains data collection sheets and forms that should be filled out with the vital information needed to enable surviving next-of-kin to handle the issues that will result as the consequence of a death in the family.

Different states and other legal jurisdictions have different laws and procedures concerning a death. Although this planning guide was written in Texas, with legal guidance provided by Texas attorneys, it can serve as a general roadmap for pre-death planning in any state or geographical location.

To avoid any potential legal issues, we suggest that you research the laws in your state, especially with regard to wills and probate and other legal documents such as powers of attorney, advance directives, and do-not-resuscitate orders.

While the content of this planning guide is relatively comprehensive, it does not, and cannot, address all of the issues that could potentially arise when a person dies. A wealth of supplemental information is available on the Internet that will provide additional information if needed. Specific administrative and legal issues unique to the situation of the deceased may require the services of an attorney or legal counselor.

REST IN PEACE

A Planning Guide for the Inevitable

CHAPTER 1

WHAT YOU SHOULD DO BEFORE YOU PASS AWAY

It is difficult for us to face the fact that one day we will die. Disturbing though it may be, however, it is essential that we contemplate what will happen to our remains and the possessions we have spent our lifetime accumulating when we are gone. By putting our personal affairs in order before we pass on, we can ensure that the property and possessions we leave behind will be distributed according to our wishes and that our remains are disposed of with dignity and honor in the manner we desire.

Few people completely prepare for their passing. Some will have taken out a life insurance policy to ensure that their survivors will not encounter a financial crisis when they are gone. Others have made no such provisions. Some will have made a will, but may not have prepared an advance directive in case they are unable to make medical treatment decisions on their own. Few will have prepared a financial power of attorney so someone of their choosing can handle their financial affairs. Even when there is a will, life insurance policies, marriage and birth certificates, and other vital records and documents, survivors often have no idea where they are located. Additionally, most people have insufficient knowledge about benefits to which their survivors may be entitled. Instructions concerning a person's desired death care services (funeral and burial) are frequently undocumented. These are all important matters to consider when putting our affairs in order before we pass on to ensure that those we leave behind will be able to deal with the details of our demise effectively and without confusion.

Because the death of a loved one often comes unexpectedly, it is almost certain to cause a major disruption in the lives of the survivors. But such an event does not have to become a crisis if you exercise due diligence and plan for your demise. What follows is a planning guide to help anyone get affairs in order before dying. It is our sincere belief that this guide will be of significant value to those who read it and complete the appropriate sample forms and templates it has to offer.

"A good plan today is better than a perfect plan tomorrow"
-George S. Patton.

Though this book might not be a perfect plan, it is a good plan. Don't delay by thinking that you'll come up with a perfect plan "tomorrow."

COLLECT AND DOCUMENT ESSENTIAL INFORMATION

Make no mistake. A death results in an information-intensive situation. A lot of data about the deceased will be needed to obtain a death certificate; make arrangements for a funeral and burial; prepare an obituary; deal with insurance companies, banks, credit unions, and brokerage houses; and obtain available death benefits. Most of the information survivors will need is available, but it is seldom recorded in one place for ready access.

The first thing that you should do to start getting your affairs in order is to collect and document your vital information. To aid in the collection of this essential information, we have provided a comprehensive and self-explanatory sample data collection worksheet in *Appendix A*. Once completed, this worksheet will contain virtually all of the essential information that will be needed by your survivors and the executor of your estate after you are gone.

WARNING

When completed, the essential information worksheet will contain highly sensitive personal data, which must be kept in a place where it is protected from compromise but also readily available to your survivors and/or your personal representative following your demise.

Appendix B provides the means for you to express your personal wishes concerning your funeral and burial services. By providing information about the type of funeral and burial services you desire, you will be removing any uncertainty your survivors may have regarding important and sensitive matters such as embalming, cremation, and memorialization.

EVALUATE YOUR LIFE INSURANCE

Taking out a life insurance policy payable to one or more of your survivors when you die is one good way of insuring that your spouse and/ or family will have a source of income to live on after you have passed away. When the breadwinner of a family dies, the income the deceased was earning stops. Unless steps have been taken to provide for your spouse and/ or family after you are gone, they may be faced with serious financial problems. There are several kinds of life insurance. Term and whole life are two of them. Each type is designed to meet specific needs. Working men and women with families may need more insurance than retirees whose children are grown and gone. The older you get, the more expensive life insurance becomes. So if you do not have life insurance, you should seriously consider it. After all, if you insure assets like your home and car against damage and loss, why not insure your most valuable asset—your life?

 If you do not have life insurance, we suggest that you talk to a reputable insurance agent to discuss the applicability and affordability of a life insurance policy; the sooner the better. It's never too late. And if you do have life insurance, we recommend that you periodically review it with an insurance agent to ensure that it is sufficient for the needs of your survivors.

Insurance policies can also be taken out to specifically assist your survivors in covering final expenses like the funeral and either burial or cremation. This type of insurance policy is readily available online and not overly expensive. You might also want to consult with a local funeral home or mortuary regarding the pre-paid death service plans they offer. See page 48 and 49.

If you are a military retiree receiving a retirement pension, payments will cease as of the day you die unless certain provisions have been made. At the time of separation from the military, all retirees are offered the option of entering the Survivor Benefit Plan (SBP). SBP is an insurance plan that requires the payment of monthly premiums based on a "base amount" or benefit level elected at the time of retirement. Full SBP coverage is based on full retired pay. Lesser coverage, if elected, can be as low as $300 per month. SBP will pay the retiree's surviving spouse a monthly annuity equal to 55 percent of full retired pay or 55 percent of any lesser base amount selected to help make up for the loss of retirement income. Not all armed forces retirees elect to participate in the SBP, and your survivors should know if you did.

If a deceased spouse was a military retiree, knowing whether or not he or she elected to participate in the SBP is key information.

CONSULT WITH YOUR FINANCIAL ADVISOR

Many people have investment programs. If you are one of them, chances are you have a financial advisor. If you are the sole owner of a regular, non-retirement brokerage account, you should consider making transfer on death (TOD) or payable on death (POD) provisions so the account can be automatically transferred to a named beneficiary (generally your surviving spouse). Your financial advisor, if you have one, will be glad to assist you.

If you and your spouse have a joint brokerage account, 50/50 ownership is assumed and upon the first death, the account will automatically become property of the surviving spouse. If you have an Individual Retirement Account (IRA), every investment house managing the IRA will require that a primary beneficiary be designated. This allows transfer to the named beneficiary upon presentation of a death certificate.

When financial resources are involved, transfer or payment requires presentation of a death certificate and instructions from the transferee. Paperwork is required to do this, and your banker and/or financial advisor can provide you with the advice and assistance you will need.

CONSULT WITH AN ATTORNEY

It is a good idea to consult with an attorney about the various legal aspects associated with your demise, especially the disposition of your possessions at the time of death. Both you and your survivors need to understand the legal documents your survivors may need. As we've mentioned, these documents include, but are not limited to, a will (*Appendix D*), an advance directive (*Appendix E*), a do-not-resuscitate order (*Appendix F*), a durable power of attorney (*Appendix G*), and a medical power of attorney (*Appendix H*).

It is not imperative that you hire an attorney to assist you in preparing your will and/or other legal documents. However, we believe that consulting with an attorney is highly advisable, especially if you will leave behind a fairly substantial estate. Most problems with estate disposition normally occur when people create their wills on their own and do not take the steps necessary to properly execute that will. In contemplating legal assistance with your estate planning and other legal matters, bear in mind that attorneys charge for their services, and the preparation of a will and/or other legal documents could cost several hundred dollars.

For documents like an advance directive, a do-not-resuscitate order, and/or medical power of attorney, you should also consult with your family doctor or a physician.

Regarding the preparation of a will, there are other less expensive alternatives to hiring an attorney. For example, online services are available, or you can purchase a do-it-yourself will kit from an office supply store. However, if you have a substantial estate (i.e., real estate, investments and bank accounts, and valuable personal property such as antiques, heirlooms, or coin or gun collections), it would be wise to retain the services of a good attorney to prepare your will. Among the things you should discuss with an attorney are the designation of an executor for your estate, how you would like your estate distributed, and the need to, or desirability of, establishing trusts and creating powers of attorney.

PREPARE A WILL

Over our lifetimes, most of us acquire possessions. These possessions— our assets or our estate (e.g., real estate, stocks and bonds, automobiles, houses, and collections of things like coins, guns, art, or antiques—can be quite valuable. What becomes of our possessions once we pass on? Who gets them? Making a will allows you to make this determination.

Preparing a will is one of the most important things you should do before you die. By preparing a will, you (a person legally referred to as a testator) 1) name one or more individuals to manage your estate, and 2) provide for the distribution of your personal and real property after you are gone. If you die intestate (without a will), the state will determine who gets your property. Almost always it will be your spouse and children, or other close relatives, starting with your brother or sister. If your relatives cannot be located, your property will go to the state. Abraham Lincoln was the most famous person to die without a will, and he was a lawyer.

A will or testament is a legal declaration. In fact, it is a person's instructions to the government (a judge) regarding how to distribute his or her property. A will can be as simple as a hand-written, signed, and witnessed document, or it can be an oral declaration.

A hand-written will is referred to as a holographic will. To be valid, a holographic will must be proven (normally by witnesses) to be in the handwriting of the testator. An oral will is referred to as a nuncupative will, and two witnesses must be present when it is made and signed. A nuncupative will is considered a "deathbed" will, meaning that it is a safety for people struck with a terminal illness and robbed of the ability or time to draft a proper written will. A nuncupative (oral) will can deal only with the distribution of personal property.

The most common will is a self-proved will. This type of will is validated by attaching an affidavit which is signed by the witnesses to the will in front of an officer authorized to administer oaths, such as a notary public. The purpose of this self-proving affidavit is to confirm that the witnesses actually saw the testator sign the will and alleviates the need to obtain affidavits from the witnesses after the testator dies.

Not all forms of a will and testament will be valid in every state. Be aware that state laws change frequently, so it would be advisable to consult with an attorney or obtain legal guidance before making your will.

When accepted by a probate court, a will is proof of the intent of the deceased to transfer his or her property to the individuals or organizations named in the will. A will is the only way that a person can "speak from beyond the grave" to ensure that his or her estate is properly settled, all taxes and debts are paid, and assets are distributed according to his or her desires. A person who has not prepared a will may have his or her estate handled by the courts rather than according to their wishes.

Whether or not you engage an attorney to assist you in preparing a will is up to you. Other services such as *Legalzoom.com* can lead you through the basics of preparing a will online. Additionally, guidelines for preparing a will and fill-in-the-blank documents are available at some office supply stores. *Appendix D* includes a will template that you may use to create your own will. Feel free to take this template with you if you consult an attorney for assistance in estate planning.

In Texas, only a properly signed and witnessed original will is valid. Copies are unacceptable. For this reason, it is smart to make *multiple originals* of the same will and place each copy in the hands of a person who has no interest in seeing them "lost or misplaced" after you are gone.

EXECUTION OF A WILL

If you choose to prepare your will yourself without consulting an attorney, be sure you know and follow the requirements of your state for executing your will (i.e., signing it in the presence of witnesses).

Generally, the requirements for properly executing a will include:

- Signing and dating your will in the presence of witnesses (two are required in Texas), and

- Having the will notarized with your witnesses present.

It is wise to choose witnesses that can be contacted after you have passed away unless you have provided a self-proved will.

Be aware that problems with wills normally occur when people prepare their own wills without legal assistance or advice.

Regardless of whether you engage an attorney to help you prepare a will or whether you prepare a will yourself using one of the variable assistance services, you definitely should prepare a will. Statistics show that more than fifty percent of people do not have wills.

If your estate is substantial and involves real estate, farm land, mineral rights, stocks and bonds, or other valuable assets, we strongly advise that you consult with an attorney to ensure that your will can be probated and your estate can be settled.

Probate and Its Purpose

Probate is a legal process conducted by a court (typically referred to as a probate court) that describes the process and procedures for transferring property from the estate of a deceased person to the parties named in his or her will. The primary purpose of probate is to determine the validity of the will of a deceased person (the testator). Probate also aids in identifying and locating beneficiaries, resolves any claims against the deceased's estate, and supervises the distribution of the deceased's assets so that the property of the deceased can be re-titled or transferred to the beneficiaries named in the will. Probate begins with a determination as to whether or not the will is valid. Probate also locates and determines the value of the decedent's assets; pays the decedent's final bills, estate taxes and/or inheritance taxes (if any); and distributes what (if anything) is left to the decedent's rightful heirs.

As a general rule, the original will must be presented for probate. Probate of a copy or duplicate of a will is not permitted unless the reason for the absence of the original will is satisfactorily explained to the court. If a properly proved copy or duplicate of an original will that has been lost or destroyed is presented to the court, it sometimes will be admitted to probate, but not usually.

Probate Procedures

Probate laws are not federal laws. They are state laws. Probate procedures are governed by state law. For details, refer to the most current Probate Code of your state. Since the 1960s, state probate procedures have been continually debated and reformed. To simplify the probate process, the Uniform Probate Code (UPC) was developed. Amended numerous times, the UPC has been adopted in its entirety by sixteen states as of this writing (Alaska, Arizona, Colorado, Florida, Hawaii, Idaho, Maine, Michigan, Minnesota, Montana, Nebraska, New Mexico, North Dakota, South Carolina, South Dakota, and Utah). The other thirty-four states, including Texas, have adopted some part of the UPC but still retain distinct procedures.

As a general rule, your property will be probated in the state in which you resided at the time of your death. If you have a stock portfolio, technically it may be located in the city where your broker maintains his/her offices. For probate purposes, however, that stock portfolio is considered to be located in the state where you lived. *Real estate is a different matter.* Let's say you live in Texas but own a farm in Kansas. This farm has to be probated in the state of Kansas even though you lived in Texas.

Proceedings

Today, probate proceedings may involve either formal or informal procedures. Traditionally, though, probate proceedings were governed by formal procedures that required the probate court to hold hearings and issue orders involving routine matters. By streamlining the process through informal procedures, the legal costs of probating an estate can be substantially lessened.

In a formal probate proceeding, a hearing must be held to establish:

- The death of the testator

- His or her residency

- The genuineness of the will

- The competency of the testator at the time the will was made

- The will's conformance with statutory requirements for its execution

These requirements are usually fulfilled by the attesting witnesses who were present at the time the will was made and who certify that it was properly executed. The number of attesting witnesses is prescribed by law. In Texas, two witnesses are required. When some or all of the witnesses to a will are unavailable, special steps will be taken. If the required witnesses have died before the testator, the person offering the will must offer proof of death in addition to evidence as to the genuineness of the witnesses' signatures and any other proof of execution available.

If fewer than the required number witness a will, it will be declared void and the testator's property will pass according to the laws of descent and distribution. In addition to having witnesses to certify the will, it is a very good idea to have it notarized.

The UPC simplifies witness issues by permitting the admission of "self-authenticating" wills. These wills contain a statement signed by the witnesses that attests to the competency of the testator and other statutory requirements. Self-authentication relieves the witnesses of the burden of appearing in court and the personal representative/executor of costly procedures if the witnesses are unavailable.

An instrument (i.e., any formally executed written <u>document</u> such as a will that can be officially attributed to its author) must be of testamentary character and comply with all statutory requirements to qualify as a will in probate. In law, a person is said to have the testamentary capacity (competency) to execute a will when that person has sufficient mental ability to know and understand what he or she is doing.

A will is testamentary when it does not take effect until after the death of the person making it. This allows the testator to retain his/her property under personal control during his/her lifetime. Even if some of the provisions in a will are invalid, obscure, or cannot be implemented, a will that has been properly executed by a competent person is entitled to be probated.

The states that have adopted the UPC provisions allow informal probate proceedings that remove the probate court from most stages of the process. In Texas, probate is notably simpler than in many other states. This is because of a provision called the independent administration of estates. Using the independent administration process, most executors in Texas are able to administer the estates for which they are responsible with very little court supervision.

In those states governed by the UPC, the personal representative (executor) must elect whether to proceed with formal or informal probate at the time of filing. If issues so warrant, a probate proceeding may be switched from informal to formal during the course of administration. Most small estates benefit from informal probate proceedings because informal probate is cheaper and quicker than formal probate.

Probate proceedings are normally held in the state in which the decedent resided or maintained a permanent residence at the time of his/her death. *However, if the decedent owned real property in another state, the will disposing of these assets must also be probated in that state.*

Informal probate proceedings generally do not require a hearing. The personal representative files the death certificate and will, along with a petition to admit the will under informal probate. The clerk of probate court reviews the submissions and recommends to the court that the will be probated. Once the court issues the order for informal probate, the personal representative files a series of forms that demonstrate that notice has been given to all interested parties about the probate, the decedent's creditors have been paid, and the estate's assets have been inventoried, collected, appraised, and distributed to the designated heirs.

The Probate Process

The probate process begins when the personal representative of the deceased (i.e., the executor of the estate or an attorney) files an action with the county clerk. Filing the probate action requires a copy of the death certificate and a petition to admit the will to probate and to grant letters of testamentary which authorize the executor, attorney, or personal representative to distribute the estate. The county clerk will then take the necessary steps to get the probate action on the docket of the probate court. Although the personal representative usually files the probate petition, it can be filed by any person who has a pecuniary interest in the will.

As a general rule, a will has no legal effect until it is probated. If the decedent leaves a will directing how his or her property should be distributed after death, the probate court must determine if it should be admitted to probate and given legal effect. A will made as a result of undue influence or fraud, or a will that has been altered to the extent that all of its provisions are revoked will be denied probate. If the alteration only revokes certain provisions of the will, the remaining provisions can be admitted to probate.

Unless otherwise provided by statute, a will must be admitted to probate before a court will allow the decedent's property to be distributed to the heirs in accordance with the terms of the will.

In general, the probate process involves collecting the decedent's assets, liquidating liabilities, paying necessary taxes, and distributing property to heirs. Receipt of probate is the first step in the legal process of administering the estate of a deceased person.

A will should be probated immediately, and no one has the right to suppress it. The person in possession of a will, usually the personal representative or the decedent's attorney, must produce it. Statutes impose penalties for concealing or destroying a will or for failing to produce it within a specified time.

The transfer of assets must go through the probate process (probate administration). However, some assets can be transferred to the new owner without probate. These include:

- Community property with the right of survivorship

- Property held as joint tenancy with the right of survivorship

- Payable-on-death bank accounts

- Life insurance proceeds

- Survivor's benefits from an annuity

The probate process results in a legal document or instrument that may be enforced by the executor of the deceased's estate in a court of law if necessary. A probate officially appoints the executor (or the personal representative of the deceased), generally named in the will, as having the legal power to dispose of the testator's assets in the manner specified in the testator's will. Through the probate process, a will may also be contested.

The probate court grants its approval by granting probate to the executor. The probated will becomes a legal instrument, and the executor named in the will is in charge of overseeing the probate process. Probate is also used if someone dies without a will (dies intestate) and the process is then needed to transfer the assets according to the default transfer plan that the state in which the deceased resided has in place for everyone who dies without a will. If the decedent dies intestate (without leaving a will), the court will appoint a personal representative to distribute the decedent's property according to the laws of descent and distribution. These laws direct the distribution of assets based on hereditary succession.

Probate Administration

As with any legal proceeding, there are certain technical aspects to probate administration:

- Creditors must be notified and legal notices must be published.

- Executors of the will must be guided by the court in how and when to distribute an estate's assets and how to take creditors' rights into account.

- A petition to appoint a personal representative may need to be filed and letters of administration (generally referred to as "letters of testamentary") issued. A grant of letters testamentary can be used as proof that the administrator is entitled to handle the assets

- Homestead property, which follows its own set of unique rules in certain states, must be dealt with separately from other assets.

In many common law jurisdictions, jointly owned property passes automatically to the surviving joint owner separately from any will, unless the equitable title is held as tenants in common.

There are time factors involved in filing and objecting to claims against the estate.

In contentious probate cases (for instance, where a lawsuit is pending over the decedent's death or where there may have been pending suits that are now continuing), separate procedures are required.

Real estate or other property may need to be sold to effect the distribution of assets pursuant to the will or merely to pay debts.

Estate taxes, gift taxes, or inheritance taxes must be considered if the estate exceeds certain thresholds.

Executors of the will must deduct the administration costs, including ordinary taxes (e.g., income tax on interest and property taxes from assets in the estate) before distribution.

Assets such as life insurance may simply need to be transferred from the deceased to his or her beneficiaries; other assets such as brokerage accounts may have pay on death (POD) or transfer on death (TOD) designations. This avoids probate.

All separate papers, instruments, or sheets comprising the most recent of a testator's wills will be admitted to probate. A codicil, which is a supplement to a will, is entitled to be probated together with the will it modifies if it is properly executed according to statute. If a codicil is complete in itself and can stand as a separate testamentary instrument independent of the will, the codicil alone can be admitted to probate. A codicil that has been subsequently revoked by another codicil is not entitled to probate.

Where a later will does not explicitly revoke all prior wills, two separate and distinct wills can be probated. Probate courts try very hard to carry out the declared intention of a testator regarding the disposition of property, and they resort to distributing property according to the law of descent and distribution only where no reasonable alternatives exist.

Some states have special proceedings to handle such occurrences. A thorough and diligent search for the will is necessary before a copy can be probated as a lost will.

A will made in a foreign language will be admitted to probate if the testator understood what it contained and it otherwise complies with other statutory requirements. A translation usually must accompany the will.

Contested Probate Proceedings

If no one objects to the will at the hearing, it will be admitted to probate. However, the probate of a will can be contested or opposed. Usually, a will is contested on the ground that the will is invalid because of the testamentary incapacity of the testator at the time he or she made the will. Probate can also be contested or opposed for non-compliance with the formalities required by the law or for any matter sufficient to show the nonexistence of a valid will. When a will is contested or opposed, formal proceedings are required.

When a will is contested, the personal representative must defend the will against attack and must employ his or her best efforts to have it sustained if he or she reasonably believes that the will is valid. In cases where the will is contested, the court is concerned only with external validity, such as undue influence, testamentary incapacity, fraud, failure of due execution, or the absence of intent that the instrument be a will. Issues of internal validity, such as violation of the Rule Against Perpetuities, must be raised in proceedings at a later stage of administration. Although a will has been probated as a genuine expression of the testator's intended distribution of property upon his or her death, if the testamentary provisions violate the law, the estate might be settled according to the laws of descent and distribution.

Only persons having some interest that will be affected by the probate can contest or oppose it. Such persons include next of kin who will receive property if the will is set aside and intestacy results, purchasers of property from the heir or heirs, administrators or personal representatives under prior wills, and the state, if there is a possibility of *Escheat*, which means that the government will receive the property if no living heirs can be found. Creditors, however, generally are not entitled to contest the will of a debtor.

Methods by which a will can be contested generally include a contest in the court having jurisdiction over probate, an appeal from the order granting or denying probate, and separate actions to set aside the order granting or denying probate.

There is no constitutional right to trial by jury in probate or will contest proceedings. Most states, however, have statutes making a trial by jury available in a will contest. Statutes usually impose time limits on the institution of will contests.

DESIGNATE AN EXECUTOR AND AN ALTERNATE

When you prepare a will, one of the most important decisions you will need to make is who the executor of your estate will be. Generally, it is advisable to designate two persons (a primary and an alternate), both of whom need to agree to serve as your executor when the need arises. Even if your first choice agrees to be executor, naming a second choice in your will is a good practice in the event that your first choice dies before you or becomes otherwise unavailable. When selecting an alternate executor, you should use the same criteria and selection process you used to make your first choice. Choosing an executor can be difficult because you want someone who is generally younger than you, honest, and competent to handle financial matters. Finding a person who meets these criteria is not as easy as it might seem.

The executor of your will plays a fundamental role in settling all matters relating to your estate. The executor is responsible for a number of actions on behalf of the testator that include, but are not limited to, filing a probate action with the county clerk, appearing before the Judge of the probate court to be sworn in, hiring a probate attorney (if necessary), protecting the estate, paying the estate's debts, distributing the decedent's property to the beneficiaries named in the will, notifying banks and credit institutions, and canceling credit cards. Most of the time, these actions will require a Certificate of Death. Death certificates are discussed in Chapter 3.

One of the jobs of the executor is to take an accurate inventory of the deceased person's assets. This includes making a list of all bank, brokerage, and retirement accounts, as well as any real property owned by the deceased. Additionally, an inventory of personal effects, such as collections, antiques, heirlooms, or other valuables must be tabulated and presented to the probate court for review.

Depending on the size and complexity of a decedent's estate and any attendant legal issues, the job of executor can be both time-consuming and complicated. Accordingly, you should carefully consider the person or persons you select to take on this duty. A spouse or another family member (son or daughter) is a common choice for executor, but some people choose a professional, paid executor. This is something that you should discuss with an attorney.

The law considers the executor of a will to be a "fiduciary." What this means is that the law imposes the highest standard of honesty and fair dealing on the executor. When selecting an executor for your estate, consider someone you implicitly trust. Be certain that you have no concerns about the honesty, integrity, competence, and reliability of the person(s) you choose to be your executor.

Remember, the executor will have access to your bank accounts, credit cards, and other assets. Consequently, the executor(s) you choose should be financially responsible. Because the executor of your will is responsible for managing your property, paying the estate's taxes and bills, and deciding whether to liquidate certain assets to cover the expenses of the estate, it is essential that you select a person who can handle money wisely. An executor who makes poor choices with respect to your money and property can seriously impact the financial situation and life of your beneficiaries.

Because of the amount of time and work involved in settling your estate, it would be wise to select as your executor a person who lives in geographical proximity to you. In settling your estate, your executor will need to access your financial papers and tax documents and may need to make multiple visits to your bank, lawyer, and accountant. If possible, choose a person who can carry out executor duties without having to travel long distances. If your executor lives far away, it may significantly slow down the probate process, thereby potentially affecting the lives of your heirs and beneficiaries.

Finally, as part of the process of selecting an executor for your will, you should discuss the role of executor with the person or persons you choose to handle your estate. Explain to them the duties of an executor. Make sure they are comfortable with their role and agree to take on the task and its responsibilities. If the person you have chosen to be your executor has any reservations or objections, or refuses to serve, you should look for another candidate.

PREPARE AN ADVANCE DIRECTIVE, POWER OF ATTORNEY AND DNR ORDER

An advance directive (also known as a Living Will and/or Health Care Directive) is a document that communicates your wishes about medical treatment to physicians and family if you become unable to do so because of injury or illness. An advance directive template can be found in *Appendix E*. By having an advance directive, you will be able to prevent confusion and relieve family members of the responsibility for making hard decisions about your medical treatment if you cannot. Without this directive, your family may disagree over what they think you would want and this could result in the courts having to become involved.

Before preparing an advance directive, you should discuss it with your family doctor and your family or your personal representative. Consider what level and type of treatment you would want, and the benefit you would derive, if you were seriously ill or injured and someone else had to make these decisions for you. Your doctor or other health care provider can provide you with resources to assist you in completing an advance directive. Once you have completed the advance directive form, provide a copy to your physician, family, and personal representative (as appropriate). We believe it is advisable to review this directive at least annually to be sure it reflects your wishes.

<u>Definitions</u>

The following definitions of terms and explanations are provided to aid you in preparing an advance directive. They should help you in selecting treatment choices that reflect your personal preferences if you cannot speak for yourself.

- Irreversible condition: An irreversible condition is an injury, illness, or disease that:
  - Can be treated but not cured or eliminated
  - Prevents the afflicted persons from caring for themselves or making medical decisions concerning their treatment
  - Is fatal without life-sustaining medical care

- Terminal condition: A terminal condition cannot be cured. It is caused by an injury, disease, or illness that, based on reasonable medical judgment, will result in death within six months, even though life-sustaining medical treatment is provided.

- Life-sustaining treatment: Life-sustaining medical treatment keeps an injured, ill, or diseased patient alive. Without it, the patient will die. Life-sustaining treatment includes medications and artificial life-support measures such as kidney dialysis, artificial breathing devices, and artificial nutrition and hydration. It does not include administration of pain management medications, medical care to alleviate pain, or medical procedures that comfort the patient.

- Artificial nutrition and hydration: This means that a patient is kept alive by fluids and nutrients provided by a tube inserted under the skin, in a vein, or directly into the stomach.

An advance directive must be witnessed by two competent adults. The witness designated as Witness 1 cannot:

- Be the attending physician or an employee thereof

- Be designated to make treatment decisions for the patient

- Be related to the patient by blood or marriage

- Be entitled to any part of the patient's estate

- Have a claim against the estate

- Be involved in providing direct patient care if he or she is an employee of a health care facility in which the patient is being cared for

- Be an officer, director, partner, or business office employee of a health care facility in which patient care is being provided

Under Texas law as well as in some other states, a person should consider preparing three other types of directives in addition to an advance directive.

The first is the **Out-of-Hospital Do-Not-Resuscitate Order.** A template can be found in *Appendix F.* The purpose of the OOH DNR is to put your wishes in writing regarding resuscitation measures in the event of injury or illness.

The second is the **Durable Power of Attorney**. A template is provided in *Appendix G.* A Durable Power of Attorney is a legal document that enables a person to designate another individual, called an agent or the attorney-in-fact, to act on his/her behalf. This document can be invaluable for your family in dealing with financial affairs and medical issues.

When you create and sign a durable power of attorney, you give your attorney-in-fact the legal authority to act in your stead, even if you become disabled or incapacitated and cannot act or make decisions on your own. Without a Durable Power of Attorney, a court proceeding is almost inevitable. If you become disabled or incapacitated, your spouse, companion or significant other, or your closest next-of-kin, will have to ask a court for authority over some, if not all, of your financial affairs.

You may give your agent as much or as little power as you wish. As a general rule, people give their agent or attorney-in-fact broad power to handle all of their financial affairs. If you make a Durable Power of Attorney, you may want to authorize your agent to do some or all of the following:

- Use your assets to pay the everyday expenses for you and your family

- Handle transactions with banks and other financial institutions

- Invest your money in stocks, bonds, mutual funds, and precious metals

- File and pay your taxes

- Collect Social Security, Medicare, or other government benefits to which you are entitled

- Manage any retirement accounts you have

- Manage and/or operate your small business, if you own one

- Buy, sell, maintain your mortgage, and pay taxes on any real estate and other property

- Buy and sell insurance policies and annuities for you

- Transfer property to a trust you've already created

- Hire an attorney to represent you in court

Your agent is required to act in your best interests, keep your property separate from his or hers, keep and maintain accurate records, and avoid conflicts of interest.

The third is an important legal document known as the Medical Power of Attorney. A **Durable Power of Attorney for Health Care** (i.e. Medical Power of Attorney) gives another person the legal right to make health care decisions for you concerning terminating medical care or ending life support measures. A template is provided in *Appendix H*. While the form in this *Appendix H* is specific to the state of Texas, ddownloadable forms of both durable and medical power of attorney are available online for all states.

Before signing a Medical Power of Attorney, you should know these important facts:

- Except to the extent you state otherwise, this document gives the person you name as your agent the authority to make any and all health care decisions for you in accordance with your wishes, including your religious and moral beliefs, when you are no longer capable of making them yourself.

- Because "health care" means any treatment, service, or procedure to maintain, diagnose, or treat your physical or mental condition, your agent has the power to make a broad range of health care decisions for you. Your agent may consent, refuse to consent, or withdraw consent to medical treatment and may make decisions about withdrawing or withholding life-sustaining treatment. Your agent may not consent to voluntary inpatient mental health services, convulsive treatment, psychosurgery, or abortion. A physician must comply with your agent's instructions or allow you to be transferred to another physician.

- Your agent's authority begins when your doctor certifies that you lack the competence or capacity to make health care decisions for yourself. Your agent is obligated to follow your instructions when making decisions on your behalf. Unless you state otherwise, your agent has the same authority to make decisions about your health care as you would have had.

It is important that you discuss your Medical Power of Attorney with your physician or other health care provider before you sign it to make sure that you understand the nature and range of decisions that may be made on your behalf. If you do not have a physician, you should talk with someone else who is knowledgeable about these issues and can answer your questions. You do not need a lawyer's assistance to complete this document, but if there is anything in the Medical Power of Attorney that you do not understand, you should ask a lawyer to explain it to you.

The person you appoint as agent should be someone you know and trust. That person must be 18 years of age or older or a person under 18 years of age who has had the disabilities of minority removed. Except in the case of a relative, if you appoint your health or residential care provider (e.g., your physician or an employee of a home health agency, hospital, nursing home, or residential care home), that person has to choose between acting as your agent or as your health or residential care provider; the law does not permit a person to do both at the same time unless the person is a relative.

You should inform the person you appoint that you want the person to be your healthcare agent. You should discuss this document with your agent and your physician and give each a signed copy. You should indicate on the document itself the people and institutions who have signed copies. Your agent is not liable for healthcare decisions made in good faith on your behalf.

Even after you have signed a Medical Power of Attorney, you have the right to make health care decisions for yourself as long as you are able to do so; treatment cannot be given to you or stopped over your objection. You have the right to revoke the authority granted to your agent by informing your agent or your health or residential care provider orally or in writing, or by your execution of a subsequent Medical Power of Attorney. Unless you state otherwise, your **appointment** of a spouse dissolves on divorce.

Once you have signed a Medical Power of Attorney, it may not be changed or modified. If you want to make changes in the document, you must make an entirely new one.

You may wish to designate an alternate agent in the event that your agent is unwilling, unable, or ineligible to act as your agent. Any alternate agent you designate has the same authority to make health care decisions for you.

This power of attorney is not valid unless it is signed in the presence of two competent adult witnesses. The following persons may not act as one of the witnesses:

- the person you have designated as your agent

- a person related to you by blood or marriage

- a person entitled to any part of your estate after your death under a will or codicil executed by you or by operation of law

- your attending physician

- an employee of your attending physician

- an employee of a health care facility in which you are a patient if the employee is providing direct patient care to you or is an officer, director, partner, or business office employee of a health care facility or of any parent organization of the health care facility

- a person who, at the time this Power of Attorney is executed, has a claim against any part of your estate after your death

All four of these documents can be extremely important in the event of a serious illness or injury. It is advisable that you discuss all of these with your physician and your family, as well as your personal representative when appropriate. In addition, you may also want to consider a directive regarding organ and tissue donations.

CONSIDER HOSPICE CARE

If you or a family member is in the final stages of a terminal illness, is expected to live no longer than six months, and has stopped receiving curative treatments, hospice care (sometimes called end-of-life palliative care) should be seriously considered.

When you choose hospice care, you have decided that you no longer want to cure your terminal illness and/or your doctor has determined that efforts to cure your illness will not be successful. This is often the case for people with cancer. Accordingly, the goal of hospice care is to provide the best possible quality of life for dying patients and their families. It is not to speed up or slow down the process of dying. Hospice care focuses not only on its patients dying as peacefully, as comfortably, and with as much dignity as possible, but also on the patient living as fully as possible until death occurs. Hospice care also concentrates on preventing and relieving pain and suffering, and easing the fear and anxiety associated with the end of a person's life.

To determine if hospice care is the right thing to do, and what level of care may be appropriate, talk with your family doctor. He or she can then contact hospice in your locale. If your doctor has any doubts, hospice staff can perform a no-cost evaluation to determine if hospice care is needed and, if so, what level is appropriate. If the family member is in a hospital, nursing home, assisted living facility, or personal care facility, discuss hospice care with appropriate facility staff or a personal care representative. Also, talk with a hospice representative regarding the family member's needs, the hospice caregivers' roles, and the hospice services available. When considering hospice care, it is very important to know and understand your options. There are times when patients require more care than it is possible to deliver within the usual scope of hospice care services. Compounding the problem is the fact that under the Medicare Hospice Benefit, a patient is no longer entitled to hospitalization benefits under Medicare Part A. Because of this, hospice provides four levels of care: routine home care, inpatient care, respite care, and continuous care. These four levels are based on a patient's needs, described below as follows:

- Routine Home Care: Hospice strives to provide an environment of care that is comfortable for both the patient and his/her family. Hospice care is usually provided at a patient's place of residence, whether he or she is living at home, staying with a family member, or residing in a nursing care or assisted living facility. Under routine care, the hospice team or care provider(s) will schedule regular (daily) home visits to ensure that the patient's medical, social, and emotional needs are met.

- Inpatient Care: When pain or symptoms cannot be controlled at home, a patient may be taken to a hospital or other inpatient care center. The patient can return home when the pain or symptoms are under control.

- Respite Care: Often, patients have their own caregivers or are attended to by family members. When these caregivers need a rest, patients can stay in a hospital or other patient care center for up to five days.

- Continuous Care: When a patient has a medical crisis and needs close medical attention, arrangements can be made for around-the-clock inpatient care in the home. The patient can return to routine home care once the medical crisis is over.

Who Is Eligible for Home Hospice Care

If you have Medicare and meet **all of the following** conditions, you are covered:

You are eligible for <u>Medicare Part A (Hospital Insurance)</u>

Your doctor certifies that you are terminally ill and are expected to live no longer than 6 months

You accept palliative care (for comfort) instead of care to cure your illness

You sign a statement choosing hospice care instead of routine Medicare-covered benefits for your terminal illness

In a Medicare-approved hospice, nurse practitioners are not permitted to certify a patient's terminal illness. However, after a doctor certifies the illness, the nurse practitioner can serve in place of an attending doctor. You can continue to get hospice care as long as the hospice medical director or hospice doctor recertifies every 6 months that you continue to be terminally ill.

What Is Covered

Hospice care includes the following services when your doctor includes them in the plan of care for palliative care (for comfort) for your terminal illness and related condition(s):

- Doctor services

- Nursing care

- Medical equipment such as wheelchairs and walkers

- Medical supplies (like bandages and catheters)

- Drugs for symptom control or pain relief (a small copayment may be required)

- A hospice aide and homemaker services

- Nutrition and dietary counseling

- Physical and occupational therapy

- Speech/language pathology services

- The services of a social worker

- Grief counseling for you and your family

- Short-term in-patient care (for pain and symptom management)

- Short-term respite care (a small copayment may be required)

Any other Medicare-covered services needed to manage pain and other symptoms related to a patient's terminal illness, as recommended by the hospice team.

What Is Not Covered

Medicare will not cover treatment intended to cure your terminal illness once you are in hospice care. If you are thinking about treatment to cure your illness, talk with your doctor. As a hospice patient, you always have the right to stop hospice care at any time in order to resume treatment.

Once you choose hospice care, Medicare will not cover any of the following:

- Drugs prescribed to cure your illness. Drugs for pain relief or symptom control are covered.

- Care from any hospice provider that wasn't set up by the hospice medical team is not covered by Medicare. Under hospice, all care that you receive for your terminal illness must be provided or arranged by the hospice team. You cannot get the same type of hospice care from a different provider, unless you change your hospice provider. You can, however, still see your regular doctor if you have chosen him or her to be the attending medical professional who helps supervise your hospice care.

- Room and board if you get hospice care in your home, or if you live in a nursing home or a hospice inpatient facility. If the hospice team determines that you need short-term inpatient or respite care services, they will make the arrangements. Medicare will cover your respite stay in the facility. You may have to pay a small copayment for the respite stay.

Unless it is either arranged by your hospice team or is unrelated to your terminal illness, care in an emergency room, inpatient facility care, or ambulance transportation is not covered. Contact your hospice team before you get any of the services listed above or you might have to pay the entire cost.

What Is the Cost of Hospice Care

With Medicare, you pay nothing for hospice care. However, you may need to pay a copayment of no more than $5 for each prescription drug and other similar products for pain relief and symptom control while you're at home. In the rare case your drug is not covered by the Medicare Hospice Benefit, your hospice provider should contact your Medicare drug plan to see if it's covered under <u>Medicare Part D</u>. If you have respite care, you may be required to pay 5% of the Medicare-approved amount.

SELECT A MORTUARY OR FUNERAL HOME AND SELECT DEATH SERVICES

The survivors of the deceased should know what death services a loved one desires so that appropriate funeral and burial arrangements can be made. The next of kin of elderly relatives should not be embarrassed to ask what a person wishes to have done following death. Does the person wish to be buried or cremated? What about organ donation and do-not-resuscitate instructions? Has an advance directive or living will been prepared, and if so, where is it located? Has a copy of the advance directive been given to the family physician or a family member? Knowing the answers to these questions will relieve the deceased's survivors of the responsibility for making difficult and stressful decisions without knowledge of the departed's wishes.

One of the certainties following any death is the fact that a mortuary or funeral home will be involved with the disposition of the remains of the deceased. Among the most important decisions to be made in planning for one's demise are those concerning the arrangements for death care services. Following the loss of a loved one, survivors require healing and closure. A funeral or memorial service such as a celebration of life is an important part of the healing and closure process. A meaningful tribute to the deceased and a means of closure for the family includes three elements: a gathering, a ceremony, and a procession to the final resting place. *Appendix B* provides a place to record your wishes regarding these events.

Use your local telephone directory or the advice of a friend or relative to locate and contact a funeral home or mortuary. If you are not sure which one is the most reputable, your church's pastor may be able to provide a recommendation. Once the staff of the funeral home is contacted, they will guide you through the death services process—including but not limited to the legal documents required, preparing an obituary, and the selection of the goods and services you desire (i.e., choosing a casket and burial plot or cremation). They can address every element of the death services available to include a funeral, internment, and a memorial service if desired. Where military veterans are concerned, most funeral homes and mortuaries are familiar with the federal and state burial benefits available for veterans and can assist the family of the deceased in obtaining these benefits. Burial benefits for veterans are enumerated and discussed in *Appendix C*.

No doubt you have seen various TV advertisements concerning the pre-purchase of death (mortuary, funeral, and burial) services. Whether or not you decide to pre-arrange and pre-pay your funeral and burial, it is highly advisable that you consult with a funeral director to determine what services a funeral home or mortuary can provide and what these services might cost.

The cost of funeral, and burial services, depending on the specific services selected, can easily run between $10,000 and $20,000 and could be more. A casket alone can cost as much as $7,000. If mortuary, funeral, and burial service are not pre-paid, the expenses will be incurred within the first few days following the death of the deceased. In Texas, burial will not take place until funeral and burial expenses are paid.

When pre-need death services decisions are made, the mortuary or funeral home you select to provide these services will file and retain your decision(s), usually in the form of a Funeral Purchase Agreement or a contract for death services. Pre-payment prevents your family from having to make complex decision at a most difficult and emotional time. Additionally, pre-planning assures that you will have precisely the kind of funeral and burial service you want, right down to the last detail. If you pre-pay, your family will not be burdened with paying funeral and burial expenses following your demise. The costs should be guaranteed and should not increase over time.

While pre-paid death services are worth considering, and there are a number of legal controls on how the death services industry can handle and invest funds earmarked for future services, caution is advised. Incidents have been reported where pre-paid funds have been mismanaged or stolen, and some funeral homes providing pre-paid death care services have gone out of business. Additionally, pre-paid services may not be refundable if you move to a new locale during your lifetime, or there may be a substantial financial penalty for withdrawing or transferring a pre-paid plan. Moreover, money paid now may not cover costs in the future (although it should), meaning that survivors could be left to cover the inflated costs.

Before a decision to pre-pay is made, it is a good idea to shop around for the most suitable, flexible, and affordable pre-planned funeral goods and services. Ask whether the pre-payment is a fixed cost or could possibly increase as costs rise in the future. Also inquire about withdrawal or transfer in the event you relocate.

If you are interested in setting aside a fund of money to pay for your final arrangements, a more prudent approach may be to contact a bank or savings institution to set up a Totten trust—an account earmarked to pay for your final arrangements. Unlike money applied to traditional funeral prepayment plans, the trust funds are easily transferred or withdrawn if need be and you have complete control over the money during your life.

The Federal Trade Commission Federal Funeral Rule

Most funeral and death care service providers have high ethical standards. They work very hard to serve the needs of the deceased and his or her family. If they did not, it is unlikely that they could stay in business. But to protect you from death service providers who are not highly principled business people, there is a Federal Funeral Rule (enacted April 30, 1984 and amended 1994) that ensures that you need purchase only the services and products you want, and that you pay only for what you receive.

This rule applies both to those discussing and/or making pre-need and at-need arrangements.

"In selling or offering to sell funeral goods or funeral services to the public, it is an unfair or deceptive act or practice for a funeral provider to fail to furnish accurate price information disclosing the cost to the purchaser for each of the specific funeral goods and funeral services used in connection with the disposition of deceased human bodies, including at least the price of embalming, transportation of remains, use of facilities, caskets, outer burial containers, immediate burials, or direct cremations, to persons inquiring about the purchase of funerals." *16 CFR 453.2,* **The Federal Funeral Rule.**

Enforced by the Federal Trade Commission, the Federal Funeral Rule requires funeral directors to provide itemized prices, whether in person or over the phone, when discussing specific funeral and burial services. Itemized pricing is not required for general, non-specific services. The Federal Funeral Rule also requires funeral homes and mortuaries to give you other information about the goods and services they provide. For example, if you ask about funeral arrangements, the funeral home must offer you a written price list that shows the goods and services the funeral home offers.

According to the Funeral Rule (www.consumer.ftc.gov/articles/0300-ftf-funeral-rule):

- With some exceptions, a person has the right to choose the funeral goods and services he/she wants.

- The death service provider must state this right in writing on a general price list.

- If state or local law requires the purchase of any particular item, the death service provider must disclose it on the price list with a reference to the specific law.

- The death service provider may not refuse, or charge a fee, to handle a casket bought elsewhere.

- Death service providers offering cremations must make alternative containers available.

While each death service component must, by law, be itemized separately, many funeral homes and mortuaries bundle their goods and services into packages that can be purchased before (pre-need) or after (at-need) death occurs. While funeral homes and mortuaries offer a broad spectrum of services to families, they are businesses, after all, and the services and products they offer have associated costs. If there are services a funeral home or mortuary does not provide (e.g., digging a grave or setting a tombstone), they will usually inform you and provide an estimate of cost.

To simplify the death service process, many of the commonly purchased items and services (e.g., embalming, a casket, funeral services, burial or cremation, etc.) are bundled into packages for easy selection. Unfortunately, it is often hard to determine exactly where the expenses lie. Ask for an itemized list of each component included in a bundled package. This is the best way to avoid unnecessary charges. Look at each item carefully and decide what you really need. Don't pay for anything you don't want or need.

PROFESSIONAL SERVICES PROVIDED BY A FUNERAL HOME OR MORTUARY

Professional services include, but are not limited to:

- Having a funeral director and staff on duty 24/7 to respond to the initial request for services

- Care and protection of the remains

- Preparation and filing of the death certificate and any necessary permits

- Making notifications to the Social Security Administration and county clerk

- Consultation with the family

- Coordination of service plans with the cemetery, crematory, and others responsible for the final disposition of the deceased

The fee for professional services includes a share of the funeral home's overhead costs that include facility maintenance, administration, insurance, equipment and inventory costs, and governmental compliance costs. Expect the fee for professional services to cost between $2,500 and $3,000.

Handling of Remains

- Embalming: Embalming is not a requirement in every state. When that is the case, it is neither necessary nor mandatory. Embalming is primarily used when the family of the deceased requests a public funeral service with an open casket. Today, open casket viewing is frequently replaced with a framed photo of the deceased so that those attending the funeral service can see (and remember) the deceased as they were in life. Embalming costs in the neighborhood of $500 to $600.

- Some funeral homes may offer the option of sealing a casket. Be aware that sealed caskets are not required by the state and do not delay or prevent decomposition. A funeral home is not allowed to make claims that casket seals will help preserve a body. This is simply is not true. Additionally, there is no state or federal law requiring a grave liner or funeral vault. Most cemeteries require them, however, to avoid having the ground eventually cave in. City cemeteries may require a grave liner or funeral vault to prevent grave vandalism. Liners or vaults may run $800 to $1,200.

- Dressing, casketing, and cosmetic services are usually associated with open casket viewing and run about $150.

- Additional preparation as the result of an autopsy or organ/tissue harvesting. Expect a cost of around $150.

- Refrigeration is necessary for un-embalmed remains and when funeral services will be delayed for more than three days. The cost of refrigeration runs about $350 to $400.

Use of Facilities and Staff

Funeral homes and mortuaries charge for facilities and staff services for visitation/viewing. This includes setup and use of the funeral parlor's visitation room, display of floral arrangements, and staff attendance at visitation/viewing. The cost is $150 to $200. Expect an additional cost of about the same amount for a rosary or prayer service at a church or another location.

Funeral homes and mortuaries also charge for the use of facilities and staff services for a ceremony in the funeral home's chapel or for equipment and staff services for a funeral ceremony in a church. This includes coordinating the funeral arrangements, supervision of the funeral, and staff to attend the funeral ceremony. The cost for this runs between $500 and $600. If you decide to hold the funeral on a weekend or holiday, expect to pay an additional fee in the range of $300. If you are a member of the church where the funeral is held, the church normally does not charge for the use of the facility.

Transportation

Transportation costs include transfer of the deceased from the place of death to the funeral home and use of a hearse to move the deceased's remains to a church and/or cemetery for burial. Expect costs to range between $400 and $800 with additional costs for mileage over twenty-five miles. Expect additional fees for the use of additional vehicles to transport family or flowers. Depending on what vehicles are used, costs can be as high as an additional $800.

Miscellaneous Services

Funeral homes and mortuaries offer, usually at an additional cost, a broad range of additional products (e.g., caskets, urns, and burial vaults) and services. These include, but are not limited to:

- Providing caskets and cremation urns

- Providing burial containers for casketed remains (e.g., vaults)

- Immediate burial

- Direct cremation

- Arranging for a minister or priest

- Arranging and handling memorial services

- Arranging and handling graveside services

- Transportation and interment of cremated remains

- Forwarding remains to another funeral home (both local and international)

- Providing other goods and services e.g., online streaming of a funeral, burial clothing, flag cases, temporary grave markers, and more

Options

It is not necessary to use traditional funeral homes or mortuaries for death care services. But all things considered, you would probably be best served by visiting a local funeral home to discuss your death care needs and the services that can be provided in accordance with your wishes.

Over the past several years, companies that specialize in the various aspects of the death and memorialization process have become prevalent. The difference between the specialty companies and traditional mortuaries and funeral homes is how they offer products and services. Traditional funeral homes require making appointments with a funeral director and visiting the funeral home, while some of the companies that specialize in cremation allow you to make death care service arrangements from your home.

All companies providing death care services must hold a funeral establishment license and are required to meet all federal and state regulations. They are also accountable for providing ethical business practices regarding security, cleanliness, and treating the body respectfully.

As with any other product you purchase, you do not have to purchase items such as caskets, urns, and burial vaults from a funeral home. Funeral homes cannot refuse the use of a casket purchased elsewhere or charge for handling it. The price of caskets and urns vary widely. It is not uncommon for those grieving the loss of a loved one to be overcome by emotion and choose a casket that is much more expensive than is needed. It is easier to choose a reasonably priced casket when the arrangements are made prior to your demise. If cremation is your choice, a large selection of very nice urns is available in the $200 to $300 range unless you plan on the urn being on display.

Today, a wide range of death service options and choices are available that offer the same quality of service at lower costs. The trade-off is that you need to do your research, ask questions, and be open to available options and alternatives. Pre-need planning will enable you to take your time and make these very important death care decisions without pressure and emotional stress.

Cremation

Cremation, as opposed to burial, is an option more people are considering. Cremation has been growing in popularity in recent years primarily because the cost of cremation is substantially lower than the cost of a traditional funeral and burial. A traditional funeral and burial, which includes a cemetery plot and internment fees can cost $10,000 or more while the cost of cremation and a basic urn for ashes generally ranges between $1,000 and $3,000.

Many mortuaries and funeral homes do not have crematoriums. As a consequence, they often outsource cremation services to death service companies that specialize in cremation. If cremation is requested and there is no public viewing of the remains, the deceased will be placed in a cooling facility until the paperwork is complete and cremation occurs.

Choosing cremation is more difficult in some states. If you are interested in cremation, do not hesitate to ask a funeral director about this service or contact a death service provider that offers cremations.

Memorial Services

As opposed to a traditional funeral, memorial services tend to have a more relaxed and informal atmosphere. This gives the family and friends of the deceased a meaningful way to remember, honor, and pay tribute to a loved one's memory.

Memorial services can be held at a home, outdoors, or at some other suitable location such as a public reception hall. If you choose cremation, there are many options available to honor your loved one. Options range from the traditional scattering of ashes to having a loved one's ashes made into diamonds or sent into space.

Other Considerations

THE OBITUARY

It is customary to write an obituary to summarize and remember someone's life and death. Most funeral homes and mortuaries will write obituaries as a service to their clients. There may be an added cost for this service.

Newspapers and other publications will accept obituaries from the funeral home or directly from the family. Since obituaries fall into the same category as advertisements, some newspapers, especially the large ones in major cities, will charge to print them.

Most newspapers will either call the funeral home/cremation service you are using to verify the death or ask that you provide a document on letterhead. A reputable funeral home/cremation company will provide this to you.

While funeral homes and mortuaries will write an obituary for their clients, the family may prefer to have it written by a member of the family or someone the family designates. No matter who does the writing, a significant amount of information about the deceased will be required to write a good obituary.

Most obituaries, regardless of how the deceased is remembered, will contain certain biographical information about the deceased. This information may include, but is not limited to, the following:

- Name and age of the deceased

- Date and place of death

- Date and place of birth (consider omitting this to avoid identity theft)

- Cause or circumstances of death (which may be omitted in paid obituaries)

- Names, relationships, and addresses (city only) of family members and when they died if they preceded the deceased in death

- Schools attended (both high school and college) and degrees earned

- Career history

- Military service (as appropriate) including highest rank held and awards received

- Club or service organization membership(s) and offices held

- Volunteer activities

- Awards won and honors held

- Hobbies and other interests (including sports)

- The date and place of funeral or memorial services including attendance restrictions such as "immediate family only"

- Any donation requests (usually in lieu of flowers) and the name, address, and account number of the recipient(s)

- The name of the funeral home or mortuary providing death care services

It is important to be factual and accurate when listing relatives or friends in the obituary. Be specific as to the relationship (i.e., do not describe the deceased's close friends as brothers or sisters or don't refer to children close to them as sons or daughters if they are not related by blood unless they are legally adopted). Doing so could present legal problems if the will is <u>not</u> probated.

In the event that a family member or someone selected by the family will write an obituary, two sample obituaries have been included.

Appendix I provides two basic obituary samples as well as a template that can be used to prepare an obituary.

As a deterrent to theft of the deceased's identity, consider NOT including the deceased's date and place of birth, last residence, and employment information in the obituary.

Other Costs

Even when funeral expenses have been pre-paid, additional costs may be incurred following a death. These include such things as purchasing a burial plot in a public or private cemetery, opening and closing the grave (which is sometimes included in the funeral home charge), and obtaining and placing a headstone. These costs should be discussed with the funeral director of the funeral home providing death services.

PAYING FOR FUNERAL EXPENSES

Pre-paying for death services may appeal to those individuals who prefer not to burden their families with difficult decisions and funeral costs. See page 48 and 49. While you don't necessarily need to pay for services in advance, you should consider the costs and make appropriate arrangements to ease the burden on your survivors. One thing you can do is set up a payable-on-death (POD) account at your bank. If you do this, you need to name the person you want to handle your arrangements as the beneficiary. These accounts don't have to go through probate and the money goes directly to the beneficiary at the time of death.

You can also ask if the funeral home or mortuary you prefer to use will accept an assignment of proceeds from your life insurance company for payment of your funeral and burial expenses. Some funeral homes/mortuaries also accept credit card payment, so you should ask what, if any, major credit cards they accept. In any event, it is important that you give advance consideration to how your death service expenses will be paid

CHAPTER 2

WHO TO CALL AND WHAT TO DO WHEN A LOVED ONE DIES

The unexpected death of a loved one can be one of the most shocking and traumatic experiences life has to offer. When a death occurs, in addition to grief, the survivors may experience confusion and unclear thinking. Knowing who to call and what to do at the time death occurs is essential. Who gets called and the actions that will ensue will vary based on location, circumstances, and cause of death.

ATTENDED DEATH

When a person dies in a hospital, nursing home, or in hospice care, the death is generally classified as attended. An attended death means that a doctor or nurse was present at the time of death and the cause of death can readily be determined. When an attended death occurs at a hospital or nursing home, the facility where the death occurred will normally make the appropriate notifications, one of which will be to the next of kin. If the deceased was in hospice care, the care provider may make the appropriate notification(s).

UNATTENDED DEATH

An unattended death occurs when a person has died alone without any witnesses available to report on the manner of death; any time a physician is not present; or when a person dies in a hospital or other facility and a physician cannot pinpoint the cause of death. (Hospice is the only exception). An unattended death needs to be reported and investigated. An investigation by authorities (usually the police, coroner, or medical examiner) is required to determine the manner and cause of death.

When an unattended death occurs, the individual finding the decedent's body must make the appropriate initial notification to authorities to obtain a legal pronouncement of death. This is done by calling 911 to report the death. When the 911 call is made, the police and EMS will respond along with a coroner or a medical examiner. In most counties in Texas, a justice of the peace, who serves as a de facto coroner, will respond.

When the authorities (police and the coroner/justice of the peace) arrive, they will investigate in order to make a determination as to the manner and cause of death. They may contact and consult with the deceased's family physician concerning any medical conditions the deceased may have had and any treatments the deceased may have been undergoing.

If there are no circumstances involved to indicate foul play or that drugs and/or alcohol may have been the cause of death, the investigating authorities may advise you to contact the death service provider (e.g., undertaker) of your choice and arrange to have the body picked up and transported to the funeral home or mortuary. In most instances, the investigating authorities will make the call for you. When an unattended death occurs, *do not* call a death service provider until the proper authorities arrive.

When a person's death occurs in a suspicious, unusual, or unnatural manner (e.g., from violence, by apparent suicide, or from some disease which might constitute a threat to public health), the county medical examiner and/or county coroner must be notified. This is also the case if a person dies suddenly when they are in apparent good health or when unattended by a physician. Notification is normally made by the authorities in attendance (i.e., a law enforcement officer, medical investigator, or justice of the peace), but can be made by any other person present.

The Texas Health & Safety Code § 671.001 provides the legal standard used to determine death in Texas. Without an investigation by authorities (police and/or a coroner or medical examiner), a determination of cause of death cannot be made. Until a cause of death investigation by the coroner or medical examiner is completed, the deceased's body cannot be released for transport to a mortuary or funeral home.

In some cases an autopsy will be required and/or a toxicology examination will need to be performed to establish the cause of death. Even if an autopsy is not required, the deceased's next-of-kin always have the option to order an autopsy through a private pathologist. This will be at their expense. If an autopsy is performed, the decedent's body will be released to the family and their funeral home of choice only after the autopsy is completed. Normally, this should not take more than a day or two.

The final results of an autopsy can take up to eight weeks, depending on the circumstances and nature of death. In order not to delay the actions that must be taken following a person's death, a death certificate certified as "pending investigation" can be obtained without a final autopsy report and before the manner and cause of death is officially determined. A final death certificate will be completed when all essential information is compiled.

In some instances, insurance companies will require an autopsy report in advance of paying benefits. Autopsy results can be obtained only through the ex-officio coroner or medical professional who ordered the autopsy. The pathologist who performed the autopsy will not release the results of the autopsy to a private party. Autopsy results will be obtained through your funeral home.

WHO TO CALL AND WHAT TO DO

IMMEDIATELY

- Obtain a Pronouncement of Death

  When a person dies, the first thing that needs to be done is to obtain a legal pronouncement of death. This should be done immediately. If the deceased died in a hospital or nursing home and the cause of death is known, the hospital or nursing home should handle the pronouncement. If a doctor was not present at the time of death, or cannot determine the manner and cause of death from care history (i.e., the death was unattended), a medical examiner, the county coroner, or (in some Texas jurisdictions) a justice of the peace who can make the pronouncement of death will need to be contacted. As appropriate:

- Call hospice

  If the deceased was in hospice care and died at home, contact the hospice nurse. He or she can make the death pronouncement and assist in making arrangements with a funeral home or mortuary to transport the body.

- Call 911

  If the deceased died at home and was not in hospice care, call 911. If applicable, it is advisable to have an Out-of-Hospital (OOH) Do-Not-Resuscitate (DNR) order in hand when EMS arrives. (See *Appendix F*). If you do not have a DNR document, EMS will generally start emergency procedures and take the person to an emergency room where a doctor can make the pronouncement of death. The exception is when a coroner is on hand or the paramedics are permitted to pronounce death. They may contact the family doctor for consultation before making a death pronouncement.

Arrange for Transportation of the Body

If no autopsy is required in order for authorities to determine the manner and cause of death, call a funeral home, mortuary, or other death service provider to pick up and transport the body. The authorities present will probably make the call for you. By law, (16 CFR 453) funeral homes or mortuaries must provide you with price information when you make the call.

Other Matters to Handle

- Notify family members and close friends.

- If the deceased had a job, call his or her employer.

  - Notify the employer of the death.

  - Inquire about benefits and any pay due.

  - Determine whether the deceased had a life-insurance policy through the company.

- If the deceased was retired military, contact the Defense Finance and Accounting Service (DFAS) at 800-269-5170 to stop military retired pay, and Veterans Affairs at 800-827-1000 to ask about any applicable survivor benefits. (See *Appendix J* for further information about survivor benefits.)

- If the deceased lived alone:

  - Notify the utilities to change billing address. (Utilities will be needed to manage the dissolution of the household.

  - Notify the post office to hold all mail until a change of address can be filed.

  - As appropriate, make care arrangements for any pets the deceased may have had.

  - Consider contacting the local police if the deceased's house is vacant, requesting that they periodically drive by and/or check the premises, if possible.

o   If the house contains valuable property, remove it from the premises, ask a neighbor to be alert to any suspicious traffic, or contact a private security provider if feasible.

WITHIN 2 TO 5 DAYS AFTER THE DEATH

- Make funeral and burial/cremation arrangements.

  o   Contact a funeral home or mortuary to arrange for death care services.

  o   Ask a friend or family member to accompany you to the mortuary.

  o   Contact a cemetery about burial/cremation.

- Determine whether the deceased had a prepaid funeral and/or burial plan. If you don't already know from information left by the deceased, inquire at both the mortuary and the cemetery chosen by the deceased. If the deceased didn't leave instructions and there is reason to believe prepaid arrangements might have been made, inquire at all local mortuaries and cemeteries if practical for your location.

- Know or determine the location of the will, birth certificate, marriage and divorce certificates, social security information, life insurance policies, financial documents, and keys/combination to any safety deposit box or home safe.

- Determine whether the deceased is entitled to any burial benefits.

  o   If the person was a military veteran who served honorably, he/she is eligible for federal burial benefits. See *Appendix C.* The funeral home or mortuary should be able to assist you in obtaining these benefits.

  o   If the deceased was a member of a trade union or fraternal or religious organization (i.e., AFL-CIO, Masons, Knights of Columbus, etc.), contact the organization. There may be burial benefits associated with the membership or the organization may be willing to conduct the funeral services.

- If the deceased lived alone, ask a friend or relative to keep an eye on the deceased's home or apartment, collect the mail, answer the phone, clean out the refrigerator, and water the house and yard plants, as appropriate. On the day of the funeral, consider having someone remain at the residence of the deceased during the service; thieves have been known to check obituaries and burglarize residences during the funeral.

- If the deceased lived alone in an apartment, contact the landlord or rental company and make appropriate arrangements to terminate the rental contract or lease.

- Cancel gym and club memberships, as appropriate.

- Prepare an obituary, or work with the mortuary or funeral home to prepare one. To deter the possibility of identity theft, it is prudent NOT to include the deceased's date and place of birth, last address, or employment.

- Check with insurance companies for-life insurance policies.

- Contact the following:

  o The deceased's life insurance company or agent

    ▪ Report the death.

    ▪ Obtain insurance claims forms.

  o Medical and health insurance companies, including Medicare/Medicaid (as appropriate)

  o Banks, credit unions, and savings and loan companies

  o Landline/cell phone, cable and Internet services, as appropriate

  o Utility companies to change or stop service

  o Post office to stop or forward mail

- Take appropriate steps to prevent theft of the deceased's identity.

  o Contact the three main credit reporting bureaus.

    - Experian: 888-397-3742 or www.experian.com

    - Equifax: 800-525-6285 or www.equifax.com

    - TransUnion: 800-680-7289 or www.transunion.com

  o Mail copies of the deceased's death certificate to Experian, Equifax, and TransUnion.

  o Mail copies of the death certificate to appropriate banks, credit unions, savings and loan companies, and other financial institutions. Include a written request that the deceased's accounts be closed or changed to joint ownership.

  o Stop any automated payments from bank accounts.

  o Report the death to the Internal Revenue Service (800-829-1040).

  o Report the death to the Department of Motor Vehicles if needed.

  o Approximately thirty days following the death, and for at least sixty days thereafter, check the deceased's credit report for any suspicious activity. (www.annualcreditreport.com)

  o Report the death to the Social Security Administration (800-772-1213) and inquire about what benefits survivors are eligible to receive, if any. Additional information regarding benefits is given below.

SOCIAL SECURITY BENEFITS FOR SURVIVORS

Survivor benefits are available to family members if the deceased was eligible for social security. Hence, the Social Security Administration should be notified as soon as possible when a person dies. In most cases, the funeral director will report the person's death to Social Security. In Texas, Social Security is notified through the Texas Electronic Register (TER), which doctors, coroners, medical examiners, and funeral directors use to enter the information that creates a death certificate.

If the deceased was receiving social security benefits at the time of his/her death, the benefits received for the month of death (no matter what time of month—i.e., 3rd or 28th) and any subsequent months <u>must be returned to the Social Security Administration</u>. If benefits were paid by direct deposit, the bank or other financial institution receiving the direct deposit will be contacted by the Social Security Administration and advised that any funds received for the month of death or later must be returned. If the benefits were paid by check, do not cash any checks received for the month in which the person died or for subsequent months. Return the checks to the Social Security Administration as soon as possible.

One-Time Payment

A one-time payment of $255 can be paid to the surviving spouse if he or she was living with the deceased; or, if living apart, was receiving certain social security benefits on the deceased's record. Payment can be made to a child who is eligible for benefits on the deceased's record in the month of death if there is no surviving spouse.

Other Benefits

Some members of the deceased's family may be able to receive monthly social security benefits if the deceased person worked and contributed to social security long enough to qualify for benefits. Persons who may be eligible for benefits include the following:

- A widow or widower age sixty or older (age fifty or older if disabled)

- A widow or widower at any age who is caring for the deceased's child under age 16 or for a disabled child of any age;

- An unmarried child of the deceased who is:

o   Younger than age eighteen (or up to age nineteen if he or she is a full-time student in an elementary or secondary school)

o   Age eighteen or older with a disability that began before age twenty-two

- Parents, age sixty-two or older, who were dependent on the deceased for at least half of their support

- Under certain circumstances, a stepchild, grandchild, step-grandchild or adopted child

- Under certain circumstances, a surviving divorced spouse

If you are the widow or widower of a person who worked long enough under social security to collect benefits, you can receive full benefits at full retirement age (age sixty-six for people born in 1945-1956), or reduced benefits (seventy percent) as early as age sixty.

A widow or widower can also switch to retirement benefits based on their own work if those benefits are higher than those received as a result of a deceased spouse's work. These benefits may be higher as early as age sixty-two or possibly as late as age seventy. The rules are complex and vary depending on each individual's situation.

Supplemental Security Income (SSI)

If you have limited income and resources, Supplemental Security Income (SSI) offers monetary assistance to low-income individuals who are at least age sixty-five, blind, and/or disabled. Even if you are not disabled, you may still qualify for SSI payments. Individuals who are over the age of sixty-five may qualify for Supplemental Security Income benefits if their income and assets are below the threshold set forth by the Social Security Administration. SSI pays cash benefits to supplement the cost of food, clothing, and shelter. If you get SSI, you may also get other benefits such as Medicaid, Supplemental Nutrition Assistance Program (SNAP) (food stamps), and other social services. Contact the Social Security Administration to apply for SSI or obtain more information.

Social Security Disability Insurance

Social Security Disability Insurance, also known as SSDI or SSD, provides income to individuals no longer able to work because of a physically or psychologically restrictive disability. SSDI does not depend on the recipient's income level, since it is based solely on work history and the degree of disability.

To qualify for SSDI, it is usually required that the applicant has worked five of the past ten years in a job (or multiple jobs) where social security taxes were withheld. If an individual receives SSDI benefits upon reaching full retirement age, the SSDI payments automatically convert to retirement benefits.

Contact a Social Security Representative

If you have not talked with a social security representative about retirement benefits (or if your circumstances have changed), contact your local social security office to discuss the options available to you.

To ensure that the deceased's family receives all of the benefits to which it may be entitled, it is essential that the Social Security Administration be contacted as soon as possible. For more information and to find copies of Social Security Administration publications, visit www.socialsecurity. gov or call toll-free at 800-772-1213. For the deaf and hard of hearing, call the Social Security TTY number, 800-325-0778. Appointments to talk with a social security representative at a local Social Security office can be made by calling the number listed in the local telephone directory.

CHAPTER 3

THINGS YOU NEED TO DO AFTER THE FUNERAL AND BURIAL

PURCHASE A DEATH CERTIFICATE

A death certificate serves as an official record of death. It is a legal document that shows the date, location, manner and cause of death for someone who has passed away. In most of the United States, death certificates are considered to be public domain documents and can be obtained for any individual regardless of the requester's relationship to the deceased.

One main purpose of death certification is to review the cause of death to determine if foul play occurred. The certification process can rule out an accidental death or a homicide based on the findings of law enforcement officers and the ruling of the coroner or medical examiner.

The death certificate provides prima facie evidence of the fact of death. Typically, doctors and medical examiners are the people held responsible for filling out the necessary forms and filing them with the state's Department of Vital Statistics. The funeral home initiates the Death Certificate electronically, and it is then sent to the certifier (physician, coroner, or medical examiner) to complete the manner and cause of death.

A full explanation of the cause of death normally includes four items:

- The immediate cause of death, such as cardiac arrest;

- Any intermediate causes, which triggered the immediate cause, such as a myocardial infarction;

- The underlying causes, which triggered the chain of events leading to death, such as atherosclerosis and

- Any other diseases and disorders the person had at the time of death, even though they did not directly cause the death.

For veterans, VA benefits are available if the cause of death is determined to be the result of a service-connected disability (e.g., a number of ailments caused by exposure to Agent Orange such as cancers and type 2 diabetes). Be sure to let those investigating the manner and cause of death know if the deceased had and/or was receiving Veteran's Administration care for a service-connected disability.

A certified death certificate is required in order for the family or executor to handle certain matters. Situations that require a certified copy of a death certificate include, but are not limited to, the following:

- Making application to obtain death benefits (e.g., Social Security Administration, Veterans Administration, lodges, fraternal organizations)

- Filing benefit claims for life insurance or insurance policies on real estate

- Probate a will

- Removal of the decedent's name in a jointly held estate

- Transfer of jointly held accounts at banks, credit unions, and savings institutions

- Transfer of the decedent's name for jointly held brokerage accounts, stock, bonds, mutual funds, and government savings bonds

- Changing titles for vehicles and watercraft

Each governmental jurisdiction (e.g., the State of Texas) prescribes the form of the death certificate and the procedures necessary to produce it. Before issuing a death certificate, government authorities normally require certification by a physician, medical examiner, coroner, or (in Texas) a justice of the peace (who is a de facto coroner) to validate the cause of death and the identity of the deceased.

Like other vital records such as birth and marriage certificates, death certificates are filed with an appropriate governmental jurisdiction—usually a registrar of vital statistics. In the State of Texas, the Texas Vital Statistics Unit of the Texas Department of State Health Services issues and retains a copy of all death certificates.

Texas uses an automated system known as the Texas Electronic Register (TER), which includes a Death Registration System. Doctors, coroners, medical examiners, and funeral homes enter information into the TER system so a death certificate can be created. The TER system also notifies the Social Security Administration of the death. In some jurisdictions, and under certain specific circumstances, a police officer or paramedic may be allowed to sign a death certificate. Usually this will be the case when the cause of death seems obvious (e.g., extreme old age) and no foul play is suspected. In such cases, an autopsy is rarely performed. This, however, varies from jurisdiction to jurisdiction.

Normally the death services provider (undertaker, funeral home, or mortuary) selected to handle funeral and burial arrangements will obtain the deceased's death certificate. The typical fee for obtaining a death certificate is $25 and about $5 for each additional copy. This cost may vary depending on the particular governmental jurisdiction involved.

It is advisable to have your death care services provider obtain between ten and twenty *certified* copies of the death certificate for use in dealing with the various situations described above.

Copies of death certificates can also be purchased online by going to *UnitedStatesVitalRecords.com*. The online Texas vital certificate processing fee is payable in advance. Payment may be made using Visa, MasterCard, American Express, or Discover credit or debit cards. The online Texas vital certificate processing fee and the relevant Texas Vital Statistics Agency fee will be charged to your credit card separately. All applications are processed upon receipt. The relevant Texas Vital Statistics Agency fee and shipping fee is payable upon review and acceptance by the Texas Vital Statistics Unit, a division of the Texas Department of State Health Services located in Austin, Texas. Cancellation or changes cannot be made after submission.

GATHER INFORMATION

To accomplish the various tasks required following a death, a significant amount of information and a number of vital records or important documents will be needed. We have included an Essential Information Form in *Appendix A* that, if completed as part of pre-death planning, should provide virtually all of the information needed in the event of a person's death. Although it will take a little time to collect the necessary data and enter it into the Essential Information Form, it will be invaluable once it's completed.

NON-URGENT TELEPHONE CALLS TO MAKE

These calls can be made following the final services for the deceased.

- Creditors

- Accountant or tax preparer to find out whether an estate-tax return or final income-tax return should be filed

- Any government agencies not already contacted (See *Appendix L*)

   o Social Security Administration at 800-772-1213 to report a death and/or inquire about benefits

   o Veterans Affairs at 800-827-1000

   o Defense Finance and Accounting Service (DFAS) at 800-269-5170 (for military)

- o   Ft. Sam Houston Casualty Assistance Office at 210-221-1702 (for military)

- o   Office of Personnel Management at 202-606-1800 (for retired civil servants)

- o   Other agencies from which the deceased received benefits, such as agencies providing pension services, to stop monthly checks and get claim forms

WITHIN 10 DAYS AFTER DEATH

- Take the will to the appropriate county or city office to have it accepted for probate.

- There is a fee for filing to probate a will. If necessary, the executor of the deceased's estate should open a bank account for the estate.

DEALING WITH TAXES

It is a responsibility of the executor or personal representative to calculate the estate taxes due or find an attorney or an accountant who can do so. Then, the executor must file the appropriate tax return to make payment. Additionally, the executor is responsible for filing a final federal income tax form (Form 1040) for the deceased. The purpose of this filing is to pay any taxes that are due on income that was earned by the deceased in the last year of his or her life, or to receive any refunds (which ultimately would be passed to the beneficiaries).

CLOSING THE ESTATE

To close the estate, the executor must prove to the probate court that he or she has notified all potential creditors of the deceased's death and has paid all bills and taxes that were due. As part of the process, the executor may also have to show releases from the state that all liabilities have been settled and provide a thorough accounting of any income earned or disbursements made by the estate after the death of the deceased.

DISTRIBUTING ASSETS

After all debts have been settled, it is up to the executor to distribute the assets to heirs according to the provisions in the deceased's will. This may mean paying funds to heirs directly, or, if the will provides for it, funding a trust for minors. While these tasks may seem easy, that is not the case in all situations. The executor may have to deal with family members or others who feel that they didn't get what should have been bequeathed to them. It is a duty of the executor to meet with the heirs and explain the distributions. In so doing, the objective is to prevent will contests that could prolong the distribution process.

ASSESS YOUR SITUATION

When a loved one has passed away and all of the details associated with the death have been taken care of, there will be time for the deceased's survivor(s) to reflect on their future. This is extremely important, especially for the spouse of the deceased, because life will be significantly different than it was.

"The reality is that you will grieve forever. You will not 'get over' the loss of a loved one; you will learn to live with it. You will heal and you will rebuild yourself around the loss you have suffered. You will be whole again but, you will never be the same. Nor should you be the same, nor would you want to." -Elisabeth Kübler-Ross and John Kessler

---

Among the many challenges following a death is adjusting to the new reality of living without the loved one. Coping with this reality may require developing a new routine, envisioning a new future, or even adopting a new sense of identity. This may require making what might be some hard and possibly unpleasant decisions. Making the necessary lifestyle adjustments does not mean that the dearly departed is forgotten or no longer missed. It simply means that the survivor(s) has accepted the situation, adjusted to it, and is allowing grief to run its course.

Several factors need to be considered in assessing a future without your loved one. These include, but are not limited to:

- Your age

- Your health

- Your financial situation

- Whether or not you have family members to take care of

Let us assume, for the sake of this discussion, that you are a spouse who has lost a husband or a wife. The companion who was your soul mate, best friend, helpmeet, and partner in life is no longer there. What will you do? Are you in good enough health to take care of yourself? Do you have a family (children or aged parents) that you must take care of? Do you have sufficient financial means to take care of yourself? How about your family? Is it possible that, in time, you may remarry? All of these factors must be considered.

For senior citizens who will be living alone, it may be necessary to consider moving into a smaller home or an apartment, living with another family member such as a son or daughter, or moving into a retirement or assisted living facility. This may mean giving up the house and neighborhood you live in and selling or giving away what you will no longer need.

Depending on your financial situation, going forward may require liquidating assets and /or finding employment. Deciding what you will need to do to move on may be difficult and stressful, but you should not be afraid of making lifestyle changes that will positively affect your quality of life and well-being going forward.

Because life goes on, it is important that it does so under your terms. As you assess your situation and your path forward in life, engage others before making any major decisions. Help is available and can come from many different sources. If you have family, talk with them. Discuss your situation with your church pastor. Consult with an attorney and your financial advisor if you have one. Don't be afraid, or ashamed, to ask close friends for their advice. They may have faced a similar situation.

NO SUBSTITUTE FOR GOOD PLANNING

Few people do everything possible to prepare for the day they will pass away. Many if not most of us will not have effectively prepared our survivors to deal with the decisions that need to be made and the situations that will arise as a consequence of our death. However, by confronting our own immortality and making preparations for our demise, we can minimize the impact of our death on our loved ones and ensure that our remains and our property are handled according to our wishes.

By making the effort to put your affairs in order before you pass on, you can ensure that your survivors are able to cope with the consequences of your demise without confusion or undue emotional stress.

By following the plans outlined in this book, you can ensure that those you leave behind will know who to call and what to do when you die. They will know the location of the important information and documents they need in order to deal with the legal and personal matters that will arise as the result of your passing. *Appendix M* provides helpful checklists for those doing pre-planning, for survivors, and for executors.

This planning guide gives you the tools and information you need to plan for your demise or that of a loved one. What you do with this information to prepare yourself and your family for your passing is up to you.

Sample Templates

In the Appendices which follow, sample templates of essential documents are provided. The actual templates are available on the website at www. confrontingdeath.com for download, completion, and printing. The code word for accessing these templates on the website is RIPtool$.

WARNING

Once completed, these forms will contain sensitive personal information. You are cautioned to protect this information from falling into the wrong hands where it could possibly be compromised.

APPENDICES

Appendix A: Essential Information

ESSENTIAL INFORMATION FORM

Vital Statistics

Full Legal Name: _____
                    First   Middle   Last

Current Address: _____
                  Street Address   City   State   Zip ode

Sex: _____ Race: _____ Social Security Number: _____

Date of Birth: _____ Place of Birth: _____
                                              City   State

Church: _____ Pastor _____

IMMEDIATE FAMILY INFORMATION

(Indicate with an asterisk (*) if deceased)

Spouse Name: _____
                 First   Middle   Last   Maiden Name

Spouse's Place of Birth: _____
                         City   State

Spouse's Social Security Number (SSN): _____

Father's Name: _____
             First   Middle   Last

Father's Place of Birth: _____
                      City   State

Mother's Name: _____
            First   Middle   Last   Maiden Name (Last)

Mother's Place of Birth: _____
                     City   State

Son's Name & SSN: _____
             First   Middle   Last   SSN
Son's Address: _____

Son's Name & SSN: _____
             First   Middle   Last   SSN
Son's Address: _____

Son's Name & SSN: _____
             First   Middle   Last   SSN
Son's Address: _____

Daughter's Name & SSN: _____
                        First   Middle   Last   SSN

Daughter's Address: _____

Daughter's Name & SSN: _____
                        First   Middle   Last   SSN

Daughter's Address: _____

Daughter's Name & SSN: _____
                        First   Middle   Last   SSN

Daughter's Address: _____

Brother's Name & SSN: _____
                        First   Middle   Last   SSN

Brother's Address: _____

Brother'sName & SSN: _____
                        First   Middle   Last   SSN

Brother's Address: _____

Brother's Name & SSN: _____
                        First   Middle   Last   SSN

Brother's Address: _____

Sister's Name & SSN: _____
                        First   Middle   Last   SSN

Sister's Address: _____

Sister's Name & SSN: _____
                        First   Middle   Last   SSN

Sister's Address: _____

Sister's Name & SSN: _____
                        First   Middle   Last   SSN

Sister's Address: _____

OTHER FAMILY AND FRIENDS

Relationship	Name	City and State	Telephone Number

HISTORICAL DATA

Date and place of marriage: _____

                                           Date   Place

Number of years in the community: _____

Occupation: _____

Most Recent Employer: _____

Retirement information (if appropriate):

- Retired from: _____
- Date of retirement: _____

MILITARY SERVICE INFORMATION

Branch of Service: _____

Service Number: _____

Length of Service: _____
From (Date)   To (Date)

Date of Enlistment or Commission: _____

Date of Discharge or Retirement: _____
Place of Discharge or Retirement: _____
Rank at Time of Discharge or Retirement: _____

Military Decorations:

- _____
- _____
- _____
- _____

Location of Discharge Papers or DD-214: _____
(See *Appendix O*)

PROFESSIONAL SERVICES CONTACTS

Attorney: _____
            Name   Telephone   E-mail Address

Accountant: _____
            Name   Telephone   E-mail Address

Investment Counselor: _____
            Name   Telephone   E-mail Address

Banker: _____
            Name   Telephone   E-mail Address

IMPORTANT PASSWORDS

Deceased's personal computer: _____

Deceased's e-mail: _____

Electronic banking:_____

Other Passwords You Might Need

Social Media _____

_____

_____

Accounts paid electronically _____

_____

_____

_____

OTHER INFORMATION

Highest Education Level: _____ __

Name of High School: _____
                              City   State

Location of College:_____
                              City   State

College Degrees Earned:

_____

_____

_____

Name of College Social Fraternity: _____

College Honorary Fraternities:

• _____

• _____

Fraternal, Civic, and Other Organization Memberships: (e.g., Rotary, Elks, Masons, etc.)

Name	Office(s) Held
Name	Office(s) Held
Name	Office(s) Held
Name	Office(s) Held

Awards Received:

• _____

• _____

• _____

Hobbies and Interests:

• _____

• _____

• _____

LOCATION OF IMPORTANT DOCUMENTS

Below is a list of documents commonly required to accomplish a number of actions required following a death. *We recommend preparing a vital documents folder that contains all these forms or placing the documents in this workbook.* Please indicate the location for each of the documents below, and be sure your family has this information.

- Certificate of Death: To be obtained from the funeral home or mortuary.

- Last Will and Testament: _____
  Location

- Social Security Card: _____
  Location

- Birth Certificate: _____
  Location

- Spouse's Birth Certificate: _____
  Location

- Children's Birth Certificates: _____
  Location

- Marriage Certificate: _____
  Location

- Divorce Papers (if appropriate): _____
  Location

- Military Discharge Papers/DD-214: _____
  Location

  (See *Appendix K* for detailed information on replacing lost military separation documents.)

- Insurance Policies:

    o Life Insurance: _____
                              Location of policy declaration pages

        ▪ _____
              Insurance company, policy holder and policy number

        ▪ _____
              Insurance company, policy holder and policy number

    o Homeowner's Insurance: _____
                                    Location of policy declaration pages

        ▪ _____
              Insurance company, policy holder and policy number

    o Automobile, Motorcycle, Watercraft Insurance (for each vehicle owned):

        _____
        Location of policy declaration pages for all policies listed below

        ▪ _____
              Insurance company, policy holder and policy number

        ▪ _____
              Insurance company, policy holder and policy number

        ▪ _____
              Insurance company, policy holder and policy number

    o Insurance Policies on Other Real Estate Owned:

        _____
        Location of policy declaration pages

        ▪ _____
              Insurance company, policy holder and policy number

        ▪ _____
              Insurance company, policy holder and policy number

        ▪ _____
              Insurance company, policy holder and policy number

    o Real estate deeds: _____
                                  Location

o Medical Insurance: _____
Location of policy declaration pages

- _____
Insurance company, policy holder and policy number

- _____
Insurance company, policy holder and policy number

- Medicare Member #/Plan Type:

_____
Location of card/coverage information

- Tricare # (SSN for active duty and retired military):

_____
Location of card/coverage information

- VA Disability Information (i.e.,
20 percent diabetes, 10 percent
hearting, 10 percent blood pressure):

_____

• Titles to Motor Vehicles and Boats:

o Vehicle A: _____
Vehicle type, VIN number and title location

o Vehicle B: _____
Vehicle type, VIN number and title location

o Vehicle C: _____
Vehicle type, VIN number and title location

• Lease/rental Contracts: _____
Location

• Brokerage Accounts: _____
Location of any paper documentation for accounts below

o IRA: _____
Bank or investment company and account number and contact, if any

o Other brokerage/investment accounts and name of
bank or broker:

- _____
Bank or investment company and account number and contact, if any

- ■ _____
  Bank or investment company and account number and contact, if any

- Bank Accounts: _____
  Location of recent statements

  - o Name of bank, type of account, and account number:
    _____

  - o Name of bank, type of account, and account number:
    _____

- Safety Deposit Box: _____
  Bank name/address, box number and key location

- Tax Returns (local, state, federal): _____
  Location of most recent returns

- Credit Cards: _____
  Location

  - o _____
    Credit card company and card number
  - o _____
    Credit card company and card number
  - o _____
    Credit card company and card number
  - o _____
    Credit card company and card number
  - o _____
    Credit card company and card number
  - o _____
    Credit card company and card number

Appendix B: Personal Wishes for Funeral and Burial Services

Gathering

A gathering allows family and friends to meet informally to give and receive love, comfort, and support from one another, as well as to pay their respects to the deceased. A gathering may include a visitation, viewing, fellowship meal, wake, informal memory sharing time, or any combination thereof.

I desire (please check, as appropriate):

__ Private family viewing

__ Public viewing/visitation

__ Video Tribute

__ Wake

__ Open casket OR __ Closed casket

__ Memorial portrait (painting)

__ Memorial picture (photograph)

__ Memorial display items (list if applicable)

__ Memory sharing time

__ Fellowship meal

Ceremony

An organized ceremony such as a funeral or memorial service offers a dignified tribute in honor of the deceased. It helps the grieving family find meaning in the loss of the loved one. The tribute may include religious or spiritual elements, reading from sacred texts, special music, eulogies, and memories of a lasting legacy. I desire (please check, as appropriate):

__ No embalming OR __ Standard embalming OR __ Eco-embalming

__ Burial OR __ Cremation

__ Specific clothing: (describe)_____

__ Jewelry (describe): _____

__ Jewelry on for ceremony OR __ Jewelry off for ceremony

__ Jewelry on for burial OR __ Jewelry off for burial*

(*If off, who does the jewelry go to before casket is closed?_____)

__ Flowers

__ In lieu of flowers, make contributions to: _____

__ Funeral service (before burial/cremation)

__ Memorial service (after burial/cremation)

__ Graveside service (before burial)

__ Firing squad and bugler if a military veteran __ Bagpiper __ Presentation of the U.S. Flag

__ Eulogy presented by: _____

__ Other Speakers: _____

__ Readings (specify): _____

Music presentation:

__ Special music: (List names of hymns or songs)

__ Recording (specify): _____

__ Soloist(s) (specify): _____

__ Chorus or musical group (name): _____

Focal point for service: __ casket __ urn __ picture (check all that apply)

Type of casket (describe): _____

OR

Type of urn after cremation (describe): _____

Burial or Cremation:

A funeral procession to the final resting place is a strong symbol of unity, support, and acknowledgement that something important has occurred. There is also finality in laying the body to rest. This provides a point of closure and gives loved ones a place to return to in the future to search for further meaning or to honor the life of a loved one.

Pallbearers (names):

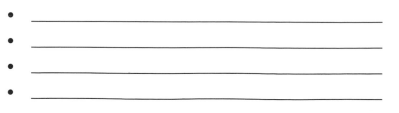

- _____
- _____
- _____
- _____

Final resting place:

__ Public cemetery __ Private or family cemetery __ National or State cemetery

Cemetery location: _____

Has a burial lot/mausoleum been purchased? __ No __ Yes

If yes, provide description:

_____

    Section   Lot Number   Space Number

Burial plot deed owner: _____

__ Steel vault   OR   __ Concrete vault

Obituary—newspapers to notify:

_____

_____

_____

Permanent Memorial Marker:

           __ Headstone   __ Marble   __ Granite   __ Upright
           __ Ground Level   __ Bronze   __ VA Headstone
           __ VA Medallion   __ Mausoleum   __ Other

Inscription: _____

_____

Other instructions (e.g., what to do with cremation ashes, etc.): _____

_____

_____

_____

_____

APPENDIX C: BURIAL AND MEMORIAL BENEFITS FOR MILITARY VETERANS, DEPENDENTS, AND SURVIVORS

All veterans discharged from the military armed services under conditions other than dishonorable may be eligible for U.S. Department of Veterans Affairs (the VA) burial and memorial benefits. Also eligible are service members who die on active duty and the spouses and dependent children of veterans and active duty service members. These benefits include:

- Burial in VA national cemeteries

- Military funeral honors

- VA headstones, markers, and medallions

- Burial flags

- Presidential memorial certificates

- Reimbursement of burial expenses

Burial in VA National Cemeteries

Burial in a VA national cemetery is available for *eligible* veterans, spouses and dependents **at no cost**. Burial includes the gravesite, grave liner, opening and closing of the grave, a headstone or marker, and perpetual care as part of a national shrine.

VA national cemetery directors are responsible for verifying eligibility for burial in VA national cemeteries. VA regional offices can assist in determining eligibility and provide you with appropriate additional information (i.e., information on state cemeteries). For assistance in determining whether a deceased veteran is eligible for burial in a VA national cemetery, contact the nearest VA regional office. You can locate the address of the nearest VA regional office in your local telephone directory under "United States Government, Veterans" or by calling 800-827-1000.

Military Funeral Honors

The Department of Defense (DoD) will provide, *upon request*, military funeral honors. These honors consist of:

- A funeral honors detail of two or more uniformed members of the armed forces

- Folding and presentation of the United States flag

- The sounding of "Taps"

Family members should inform their funeral director if they want military funeral honors. The Department of Defense (DoD) maintains a toll-free number, 877-MILHONR (1- 877-645-4667), for use only by funeral directors to request military funeral honors.

The VA can help arrange honors for burials at VA national cemeteries. Veterans' service organizations or volunteer groups may help provide honors. For more information, visit www.militaryfuneralhonors.osd.mil/.

VA Headstones, Markers and Medallions

Headstones and Markers

Veterans, active duty service members, and retired reservists and National Guard service members are eligible for an inscribed headstone or marker for their unmarked grave at any cemetery—national, state veterans, tribal, or private. Upon request, and at no charge to the applicant, the VA will deliver a headstone or marker anywhere in the world, regardless of the date of death. Headstones or markers for VA national cemeteries, a state veterans' cemetery, or a military post/base cemetery will be ordered by the cemetery director using inscription information provided by the next of kin or authorized representative.

Spouses and dependent children are eligible for a government headstone or marker only if they are buried in a national or state veterans' cemetery.

Upright headstones come in granite or marble. They are 42 inches long, 13 inches wide and 4 inches thick. Weight is approximately 230 pounds. Flat markers are available in bronze, granite or marble. Bronze markers are 24 inches long, 12 inches wide and have a 3/4 inch rise. Weight is approximately 18 pounds. Anchor bolts are provided. Flat granite or marble grave markers are 24 inches long, 12 inches wide and 4 inches thick. They weigh approximately 130 pounds. The style provided will be consistent with existing monuments at the place of burial.

Inscriptions

All headstones and markers furnished by the government must be inscribed with the legal name of the deceased, his or her branch of service, and years of birth and death in this order. *If space is available*, the inscription may contain optional information to include all of the following:

- An emblem of belief

- Military rank

- War service (e.g., "Vietnam")

- Complete dates of birth and death

- Military decorations and awards

- Military organizations

- Civilian or veteran affiliations

- Personalized words of endearment

All inscriptions will be in English.

Niche Markers

Niche markers are available to mark columbaria used for internment of cremated remains. These markers are 8 1/2 inches long and 5 1/2 inches wide with a 7/16 rise. Mounting bolts are furnished with the marker.

Medallions

The VA has authority to furnish, upon request, a medallion or other device to signify the deceased's status as a veteran. These are designed to be affixed to a headstone or marker furnished at private expense. Medallions are made of bronze and are available in 3 sizes: 5 inches, 3 inches, and 1½ inches. Each medallion will be inscribed with the word *VETERAN* across the top and the branch of service at the bottom.

Headstones, markers, and medallions previously furnished by the government may be replaced at the government's expense if badly deteriorated, illegible, vandalized, or stolen.

VA Headstones or Markers for Private Cemeteries

Before ordering a headstone or marker for a private cemetery, the next of kin or authorized representative should check with the cemetery to ensure that the government-furnished headstone or marker will be accepted. All installation fees at private cemeteries are the responsibility of the applicant.

To submit a claim for a headstone or marker for a gravesite in a private cemetery, use VA Form 40-1330, Application for Standard Government Headstone or Marker (available at http://www.va.gov/vaforms/). A copy of the veteran's military discharge document or DD-214 is required. Completed forms should be mailed to Memorial Programs Service, Department of Veterans Affairs, 5109 Russell Road, Quantico, VA 22134-3903. The form and supporting documents may also be faxed toll free to 800-455-7143.

Additional Information

To check the status of a claim for a headstone or marker for placement in a national, state, or tribal veterans' cemetery, please call the cemetery. To check the status of one being placed in a private cemetery, please contact the Applicant Assistance Unit at 800-697-6947 or via email at mps.headstone@va.gov.

In the state of Texas, additional information about burial benefits for veterans, including eligibility, headstones and markers, and burial flags can be obtained by contacting the Texas Veterans Commission, P.O. Box 12277, Austin, Texas 78711-2277 and requesting a copy of a booklet entitled, Federal and State of Texas Burial Benefits for Veterans, Dependents, and Survivors. The Texas Veterans Commission maintains an office at 5788 Eckhert Road, San Antonio, TX, Tel. 210-699-5076. Similar offices are available in each state.

Burial Flags

To honor the memory of veterans who served honorably in the U.S. Armed Forces, a United States flag is provided free of charge by the VA to drape a deceased veteran's coffin or accompany his or her urn. Also eligible for a burial flag are veterans who were entitled to retired pay for service in the Reserves or National Guard, or would have been entitled if over age sixty; and members or former members of the Selected Reserve who served their initial obligation, or were discharged for a disability incurred or aggravated in the line of duty, or died while a member of the Selected Reserve.

Flags can be obtained at any VA Regional Office or U.S. Post Office by completing VA Form 27-2008, Application for United States Flag for Burial Purposes. A copy of VA Form 27-2008 can be found online at http://www.vba.va.gov/pubs/forms/VBA-27-2008-ARE.pdf

Funeral Directors will usually help the family of the deceased in obtaining a burial flag.

After the funeral or internment service, the burial flag is normally presented to the next-of-kin of the deceased veteran as a keepsake. Where there is no next-of-kin, the VA will give the flag to a friend who makes a request for it. In VA national cemeteries having an Avenue of Flags, the family of a veteran buried there may donate the burial flag of their loved one to be flown on patriotic holidays.

Presidential Memorial Certificate

A Presidential Memorial Certificate (PMC) is an engraved paper certificate, signed by the current President of the United States, to honor the memory of honorably discharged deceased veterans. Next of kin, relatives, or other loved ones *may apply* for a certificate by mailing or faxing a completed and signed VA Form 40-0247, Presidential Memorial Certificate Request Form (available at http://www.va.gov/vaforms/), along with a copy of the veteran's DD 214, military discharge documents, or proof of honorable military service. The processing of requests sent without supporting documents will be delayed until eligibility can be determined. Eligibility requirements can be found at www.cem.va.gov.

Reimbursement of Burial Expenses

For the purpose of funeral and burial benefits eligibility, *it is important to know if a discharged or retired veteran had a service-connected disability.* Some benefits are available only if the veteran had a service-connected disability. If the deceased veteran did have a service-connected disability, this should be discussed with the attending physician or the medical examiner/coroner at the time of death and prior to completion of a death certificate.

Funeral and Burial Allowance

For a veteran whose death was service-connected, the VA will pay a funeral and burial allowance up to $2,000.* Also, in some cases, VA will pay the cost of transporting the remains of a veteran whose death was service-connected to the nearest national cemetery with available gravesites. When a veteran dies and the cause of death can be established as service-connected, the person who bore the veteran's burial expenses may claim reimbursement from the VA if the cause of death was service connected. There is no time limit on claiming reimbursement.

Burial and Plot Allowances for Internment in a Private Cemetery

For burial in a private cemetery, the VA will provide $300* for burial expenses and $722* as a plot allowance if the service member is buried in a cemetery not under U.S. government jurisdiction and the veteran was discharged from active service due to a *service-connected disability*; was eligible to receive a pension or compensation for a service-connected disability; or died in a VA facility, a VA-contracted nursing home or a state veterans nursing home.

The plot allowance may be paid to the state for the cost of a plot or interment in a state-owned cemetery reserved solely for veteran burials if the veteran is buried without charge. Burial expenses paid by the deceased's employer or a state agency will not be reimbursed.

*Prices are current as of this writing but subject to change at any time.

Appendix D: Last Will and Testament Template

LAST WILL AND TESTAMENT OF

_____
Full legal name of testator

I, _____, presently residing at _____
   Full legal name of testator

_____
Complete street address, city, state and zip code

declare that this is my Last Will and Testament. In making this will, I declare that I am of sound mind and legal age. All previous Wills are hereby revoked.

I am presently married to _____.
                          Full legal name of spouse

I have __ living children whose names, dates of birth, and current addresses are as follows:

- _____
   Full legal name   Date of birth

   _____
   Current street address, city, state and zip code

- _____
   Full legal name   Date of birth

   _____
   Current street address, city, state and zip code

I have __ living grandchildren whose names, dates of birth, and current addresses are as follows:

- _____
  Full legal name   Date of birth

  _____
  Current street address, city, state and zip code

- _____
  Full legal name   Date of birth

  _____
  Current street address, city, state and zip code

Note: Use additional pages as necessary to list all children and grandchildren.

From my estate I make these specific gifts:

1. To _____ I give the following:
   Full legal name of individual or organization

   _____
   Complete description of item or property given

2. To _____ I give the following:
   Full legal name of individual or organization

   _____
   Complete description of item or property given

3. To _____ I give the following:
   Full legal name of individual or organization

   _____
   Complete description of item or property given

4. To _____ I give the following:
   Full legal name of individual or organization

Page __ of __ pages   Testator's initials _____

Complete description of item or property given

5. To _____ I give the following:
   Full legal name of individual or organization

Complete description of item or property given

6. To _____ I give the following:
   Full legal name of individual or organization

Complete description of item or property given

7. To _____ I give the following:
   Full legal name of individual or organization

Note: Use additional pages as necessary.

Page __ of __ pages   Testator's initials _____

All of the rest of my property, whether real or personal, and regardless of where it is located, I give to _____
who is my _____. Full legal name of individual or organization
                    Specify relationship

Any property, whether real or personal, acquired by me subsequent to the making of this Will I also leave to _____
who is my _____. Full legal name of individual or organization
                    Specify relationship

If the person or organization named is not surviving, my property, whether real or personal, regardless of where it is located, shall go to _____ who is my _____.

Full legal name or individual or organization   Specify relationship

All of the beneficiaries I have named in this Will must survive me by thirty (30) days in order to receive any gift under this Will. In the event that any beneficiary and I die simultaneously, I shall be presumed to have survived that beneficiary for the purposes of this Will.

To serve without bond as the Executor of my estate, I appoint my

_____,

Specify relationship

_____, who has been notified of this appointment,

Full legal name of Executor

has agreed to serve, and presently resides at the following address:

_____.

Current street address, city, state and zip code

If my appointed Executor does not survive me or is in any way unable to serve, I appoint as Alternate Executor of my estate, to serve without bond, my _____,

Specify relationship

_____, who has been notified of this appointment,

Full legal name of Alternate Executor

has agreed to serve, and presently resides at the following address:

_____

In addition to any powers, authority, and discretion granted by law, I give to my Executor and Alternate Executor the authority, and all necessary power to pursue independent administration, and to act, with or without court approval, at his or her sole discretion, to independently manage and administer my estate and distribute my property, whether real or personal, in accordance with this Will.

By affixing my signature and name below, I hereby publish this Last Will and Testament, consisting of __ typewritten pages on this _____ day of _____ in the year _____, I declare that I do this

    Day   Month   Year

freely and of my own accord for the purposes expressed herein. I attest that I am of sound mind and legal age and under no undue influence, coercion, or constraint at the time of the making of this Will.

_____   _____

Printed name of the testator   Signature of the testator

Self-Proving Affidavit

Having first been sworn to oath, and under penalty of perjury, we the undersigned state that on _____, the above named testator, in the presence of us all, did Day   Month   Year

publish and sign this Last Will and Testament.

In the testator's presence, at the testator's request, and in the presence of us all, we have signed below as witnesses and declare, under penalty of perjury, that to the best of our knowledge, the testator who signed this document was of sound mind and legal age and under no undue influence, coercion, or constraint.

_____   _____

Printed name of first witness   Signature of first witness

_____   _____

Printed name of second witness   Signature of second witness

Notary Public Certification:

On _____ in the State of _____, County of _____, the testator,

        Day   Month   Year

_____, and three witnesses, _____,

        Name of Testator   Name of Witness

_____, and _____,

        Name of Witness   Name of Witness

personally appeared before me, and being duly sworn, did state that they are the persons described in the above document and that they freely and voluntarily, without reservation, signed this document for the purposes stated.

_____   _____
Printed Name of Notational Officer   Signature of Notational Officer

I am a Notary Public in the County of _____, State of _____. My ommission expires _____.

                Day   Month   Year

Notary Seal

Page ___ of ___ pages   Testator's initials _____

Appendix E: Advance Directive

ADVANCE DIRECTIVE

I, _____, recognize that the best health care is
Full Legal Name based upon a partnership of trust

and communication with my physician. As long as I am of sound mind
and able to make my wishes known, I and my physician will make my
health care decisions together. If there comes a time that I am unable
to make medical decisions about myself because of illness or injury, **I
direct that the following treatment preferences be honored.** If, in the
judgment of my physician, I am suffering with a terminal condition
from which I am expected to die within six months, even with available
life-sustaining treatment provided in accordance with prevailing standards
of medical care, I hereby request that (*initial one of the two choices below*):

_____ All treatments other than those needed to keep me comfortable
be discontinued or withheld and my physician allow me to die as gently
as possible.

OR

_____ I be kept alive in this terminal condition using available life-sustaining
treatment.

(THIS SELECTION DOES NOT APPLY TO HOSPICE CARE.)

If, in the judgment of my physician, I am suffering with an irreversible
condition so that I cannot care for myself or make decisions for myself
and am expected to die without life-sustaining treatment provided in
accordance with prevailing standards of care, I hereby request that (*initial
one of the two choices below*):

_____All treatments other than those needed to keep me comfortable be discontinued or withheld and my physician allow me to die as gently as possible.

OR

_____ I be kept alive in this irreversible condition using available life-sustaining treatment. *(THIS SELECTION DOES NOT APPLY TO HOSPICE CARE.)*

Additional requests: *(After discussion with your physician, you may wish to consider listing particular treatments in the space below that you do or do not want in specific circumstances, such as artificial nutrition and fluids, intravenous antibiotics, etc.)*

_____

_____

_____

(Be sure to state whether you do or do not want the particular treatment.)

After signing this directive, if my personal representative or I elect hospice care, I understand and agree that only those treatments needed to keep me comfortable would be provided and I would not be given available life-sustaining treatments.

If I do not have a Medical Power of Attorney, and I am unable to make my wishes known, I designate the following person(s) to make treatment decisions with my physician compatible with my personal values:

1. _____

                 Person's Name

2. _____

                 Person's Name

(NOTE: If a Medical Power of Attorney has been executed, then an agent already has been named and you should not list additional names in this document.)

If the above persons are not available, or if I have not designated a spokesperson, I understand that a spokesperson will be chosen for me following standards specified in the laws of Texas (or use the state where you currently reside). If, in the judgment of my physician, my death is imminent within minutes to hours, even with the use of all available medical treatment provided within the prevailing standard of care, I acknowledge that all treatments may be withheld or removed except those needed to maintain my comfort. **I understand that under Texas law this directive has no effect if I have been diagnosed as pregnant.** This directive will remain in effect until I revoke it. No other person may do so.

Signed _____ Date _____

City, County, and State of Residence _____

We, the undersigned, hereby acknowledge the signature of the declarant.

Witness 1: _____

Witness 2: _____

Appendix F: Do-Not-Resuscitate Order

OUT-OF-HOSPITAL (OOH) DO-NOT-RESUSCITATE (DNR) ORDER

This document (order) becomes effective immediately on the date of execution for health care professionals acting in out-of-hospital settings. It remains in effect until the person named below (the declarant) is pronounced dead by authorized medical or legal authority or the document is revoked. Comfort care will be given as needed. **A copy of this document must accompany the person during his/her transport.**

Declarant's Legal Name_____

                                      First   Middle   Last

Date of Birth: _____Sex (choose one): _____ Male _____ Female

                    mm/dd/yyyy

SSN: _____

        Social Security Number

A. Declaration of the adult person named above: I am competent and at least 18 years of age. I direct that none of the following resuscitation measures be initiated or continued for me: a) cardiopulmonary resuscitation (CPR); b) transcutaneous cardiac pacing; c) defibrillation, d) advanced airway management; and /or e) artificial ventilation.

_____ _____ _____

Signature   Date (mm/dd/yyyy)   Printed Name

B. Declaration by legal guardian, agent, or proxy on behalf of the adult person named above who is incompetent or otherwise incapable of communication: I am the (__legal guardian), (__agent in a Medical Power of Attorney), or (__proxy in a directive to physicians of the above named person who is incompetent or otherwise mentally or physically incapable of communication). Based on the known desires of the person named above, or a determination of the best interests of that person, **I direct that none of the following resuscitation measures be initiated or continued for the person**: a) cardiopulmonary resuscitation (CPR); b) transcutaneous cardiac pacing; c) defibrillation, d) advanced airway management; and /or e) artificial ventilation.

_____   _____   _____

Signature   Date (mm/dd/yyyy)   Printed Name

C. Declaration by a qualified relative of the adult person named above who is incompetent or otherwise incapable of communication and is without legal guardian, agent, or proxy. Based on the known desires of the person named above, or a determination of the best interests of that person, **I direct that none of the following resuscitation measures be initiated or continued for the person**: a) cardiopulmonary resuscitation (CPR); b) transcutaneous cardiac pacing; c) defibrillation, d) advanced airway management; and /or e) artificial ventilation.

_____   _____   _____

Signature   Date (mm/dd/yyyy)   Printed Name

D. Declaration by physician based on directive to physicians by a person now incompetent or non-written communication to the physician by a competent person: I am the attending physician of the adult person named above and have (__ seen evidence of his/her previously issued directive to physicians by the adult now incompetent), or (__ observed his/her issuance before two witnesses of an OOH-DNR in a non-written manner).

I direct that none of the following resuscitation measures be initiated or continued for the person: a) cardiopulmonary resuscitation (CPR); b) transcutaneous cardiac pacing; c) defibrillation, d) advanced airway management; and /or e) artificial ventilation.

_____   _____   _____

Signature   Date (mm/dd/yyyy)   Printed Name

Two Witnesses: We have witnessed the above named competent adult person or authorized declarant making his/her signature above and, if applicable, the above named adult person making an OOH-DNR by non-written communication to the attending physician.

Witness 1 Signature:

_____   _____   _____

Witness Signature   Date (mm/dd/yyyy)   Printed Name

Witness 2 Signature:

_____   _____   _____

Witness Signature   Date (mm/dd/yyyy)   Printed Name

Notary Public Certification:

On _____ in the State of _____, County of _____, the declarant

Day   Month   Year

_____, and two witnesses, _____ and

Name of Declarant   Name of Witness 1

_____, personally appeared before me, and being duly

Name of Witness 2   sworn, did state that they are

the persons described in the above document and that they freely and voluntarily, without reservation, signed this document for the purposes stated.

_____   _____

Signature of Notational Officer   Printed Name of Notational Officer

I am a Notary Public in the County of _____, State of _____.

My Commission expires _____   Notary Seal

Day   Month   Year

All persons who have signed above must sign below acknowledging that this document has been properly completed.

_____ _____   _____   _____

Signature of Declarant   Signature of guardian/agent/proxy/relative   Signature of Attending Physician

_____   _____   _____

Signature of Witness 1   Signature of Witness 2   Notary's Signature

Appendix G: Durable Power of Attorney

TEXAS STATUTORY DURABLE POWER OF ATTORNEY

The powers granted by this document are explained in the Durable Power of Attorney Act, Chapter XII, Texas Probate Code.

This document does not authorize anyone to make medical or other health care decisions for me, and I may revoke this Power of Attorney at a later date if I wish to do so.

I, _____

   First Name   Middle Name   Last Name

_____

  Street Address   City   State   Zip Code

do hereby appoint _____

     First Name   Middle Name   Last Name

as my agent (attorney-in-fact) to act for me in any lawful way with respect to all of the following powers enumerated below except for those powers that I have withheld and crossed out below:

- Real property transactions

- Tangible personal property transactions

- Stock and bond transactions

- Commodity and option transactions

- Banking and other financial institution transactions

- Business operating transactions

- Insurance and annuity transactions

- Estate, trust, and other beneficiary transactions

- Claims and litigation

- Personal and family maintenance

- Benefits from social security, Medicare, Medicaid, or other governmental programs or civil or military service

- Retirement plan transactions

- Tax matters

IF NO POWER LISTED ABOVE IS CROSSED OUT, THIS DOCUMENT SHALL BE CONSTRUED AND INTERPRETED AS A GENERAL POWER OF ATTORNEY AND MY AGENT (ATTORNEY-IN-FACT) SHALL HAVE THE POWER AND AUTHORITY TO PERFORM OR UNDERTAKE ANY ACTION I COULD PERFORM OR UNDERTAKE IF I WERE PERSONALLY PRESENT.

SPECIAL INSTRUCTIONS:

On the lines below are my special instructions limiting or extending the powers granted to my agent:

_____

_____

_____

_____

<u>Special instructions applicable to gifts</u>:

_____ I grant my agent (attorney in fact) the power to apply my
Initial here   property to make gifts, except

that the amount of a gift to any individual may not exceed the amount of annual exclusions allowed from the federal gift tax for the calendar year of the gift.

Unless I direct otherwise above, this Power of Attorney is effective immediately and will continue until it is revoked.

CHOOSE ONE OF THE FOLLOWING ALTERNATIVES BY CROSSING OUT THE ALTERNATIVE NOT CHOSEN:

(A) This power of attorney is not affected by my subsequent disability or incapacity.

- By choosing this alternative, this Power of Attorney is to become active on the date it is executed.

(B) This power of attorney becomes effective upon my disability or incapacity.

- By choosing this alternative (and a definition of my disability or incapacity is not contained in this Power of Attorney), I shall be considered disabled or incapacitated for the purposes of this Power of Attorney if a physician certifies in writing at a date later than the date this Power of Attorney is executed that, based on the physician's medical examination of me, I am mentally incapable of managing my financial affairs.

- I authorize the physician who examines me for this purpose to disclose my physical or mental condition to another person for purposes of this Power of Attorney.

Note: If neither (A) or (B) above is crossed out, it will be assumed that I have chosen (A).

A third party who accepts this Power of Attorney is fully protected from any action taken under this Power of Attorney that is based on the determination made by a physician of my disability or incapacity. I agree that any third party who receives a copy of this document may act under it. Revocation of the Durable Power of Attorney is not effective as to a third party until the third party receives actual notice of the revocation. I agree to indemnify the third party for any claims that arise against the third party because of reliance on this Power of Attorney.

If any agent named by me dies, becomes legally disabled, resigns, or refuses to act, I name the following (each to act alone and successively, in the order named) as successor(s) to that agent:

Page __ of __ pages   Preparer's initials _____

_____

Full legal name   Address   Telephone

_____

Full legal name   Address   Telephone

Signed this _____ day of _____, 20___ in the State of _____

County of _____.

_____

Signature

Notary Acknowledgement:

This document was acknowledged before me on _____

                                             Day   Month   Year

by _____

Name of Principal

_____

Printed Name of Notational Officer   Signature of Notational Officer

My commission expires: _____

                    Day   Month   Year

                                                    Notary Seal

By accepting or acting under this appointment, the Attorney-in-Fact or Agent assumes the fiduciary and other legal responsibilities of an agent.

Page ___ of ___ pages   Preparer's initials _____

APPENDIX H: MEDICAL POWER OF ATTORNEY

MEDICAL POWER OF ATTORNEY

(See Advance Directives Act (§166.164, Texas Health and Safety Code)

Designation of Health Care Agent:

I, _____

        Full legal name   Complete Address   Telephone

appoint _____ as my agent to make any and all health care

        Full legal name

decisions for me, except to the extent I state otherwise in this document.

If the agent designated above is my spouse, the designation is automatically revoked by law if the marriage is dissolved.

If the person designated as my agent is unable or unwilling to make health care decisions for me, I designate the following person(s), in order, to serve as my alternate agent(s) to make health care decisions for me as authorized by this document.

_____

        Full legal name   Address   Telephone

_____

        Full legal name   Address   Telephone

Page ___ of ___ pages   Preparer's initials _____

This Medical Power of Attorney takes effect if I become unable to make my own health care decisions and the fact that I am unable to do so is certified in writing by my physician.

Limitations on the decision-making authority of my agent are as follows:

_____

_____

The original of the document is kept at _____.

The following individuals or institutions possess signed copies of this Medical Power of Attorney:

1. _____

       Name   Address   Telephone

2. _____

       Name   Address   Telephone

The following individuals or institutions have signed copies of this Medical Power of Attorney:

_____

       Name   Address   Telephone

_____

       Name   Address   Telephone

Page ___ of ___ pages   Declarant's initials_____

Duration:

I understand that this Power of Attorney exists indefinitely from the date I execute this document unless I establish a shorter time or revoke the power of attorney. If I am unable to make health care decisions for myself when this Power of Attorney expires, the authority I have granted my agent continues to exist until the time I become able to make health care decisions for myself. (If Applicable) This Power of Attorney ends on the following date: _____

Prior Designations Revoked

I revoke any prior medical power of attorney.

Acknowledgement of Disclosure Statement

I have been provided with a disclosure statement explaining the effect of this document. I have read and understand the information contained in this disclosure statement.

I sign my name to this Medical Power of Attorney on _____, in the City of

Date (mm/dd/yyyy)

_____, in _____ County, in the State of _____

_____   _____   _____

Declarant's Signature   Date (mm/dd/yyyy)   Declarant's Printed Name

Statement of Witnesses

I am not the person appointed as agent by this document. I am not related to the principal by blood or marriage. I would not be entitled to any portion of the principal's estate upon the principal's death. I am not the attending physician of the principal or an employee of the attending physician. I have no claim against any portion of the principal's estate on the principal's death. Furthermore, if I am an employee of a health care facility in which the principal is a patient, I am not involved in providing direct patient care to the principal and am not an officer, director, partner, or business office employee of the health care facility or of any parent organization of the health care facility.

Page ____ of ____ pages   Declarant's initials_____

We, the undersigned, hereby acknowledge the signature of the declarant.

Witness 1: _____

Witness 2: _____

Notary Acknowledgement:

This document was acknowledged before me on _____

Date (mm/dd/yyyy)

by _____

Name of Principal

Signed this ____ day of _____, 20___ in the State of _____,

County of _____.

_____   _____
Printed Name of Notational Officer   Signature of Notational Officer

My commission expires: _____

Date (mm/dd/yyyy)

Notary Seal

Page ____ of ____ pages   Declarant's initials_____

Appendix I: Obituaries—Samples and Templates

Sample Obituary #1

Elizabeth "Ellie" Smith (née Robinson) died peacefully at the age of 84 at her home in Dime Box, Texas, on October 30, 2014 due to complications of diabetes.

A native Texan, Elizabeth was born on April 1, 1930, in Giddings, Texas, to her parents, Herbert and Betty Sue Robinson. "Miss Ellie," as she was called by her friends and later the students she taught, grew up and attended elementary and high school in Dime Box. She was a high school cheerleader and played violin in the school orchestra.

Elizabeth graduated from Texas Tech University in Lubbock, Texas, with a degree in Elementary Education in 1954. After graduation, she took a teaching position at Dory Miller Middle School in Dime Box and taught seventh grade until her retirement in 1994. She received three Dime Box "Best Elementary School Teacher" Awards and was named Texas Elementary School Teacher of the Year in 1982.

In 1956, Elizabeth married William Smith of College Station, Texas. William, a graduate of Texas A&M University, owned and managed the Dime Box Feed and Supply Company. Ellie and William had one daughter, Jessica, who was born in 1958, and one son, Robert, who was born in 1960. Jessica followed her mother in the teaching profession and presently teaches mathematics at Travis High School in Austin, TX. Robert works for the National Security Agency in Washington, D.C.

"Miss Ellie" will be fondly remembered as a patient and supportive teacher with a passion for literacy, music, and the arts. An accomplished musician, Mrs. Smith gave voice and piano lessons to young students and sang in the River Bend Church Choir and Dime Box Community Chorus.

Mrs. Smith is survived by her daughter and son-in-law, Jessica and James Wilson of Austin, Texas; her son, Robert Smith; her brother, Raymond Robinson; and four grandchildren. She is preceded in death by her husband, William, and her sister, Betty.

Mrs. Smith will be buried following a private ceremony at the Prairie View Cemetery on November, 4, 2014. A memorial service will take place on Sunday, November 7, at 3:00 p.m. at Friendship Hall. All are welcome to attend and celebrate Mrs. Smith's life. In lieu of flowers, the family asks that donations please be made to the River Bend Methodist Church Choir, PO Box 123, Dime Box, TX 77777, or the American Diabetes Association.

Sample Obituary #2

Ronald Honas "Ron" James passed away Friday, December 6, 2014, at the age of 79.

Born in Hoxie, Kansas, in 1935 to Herbert and Louise James, Ron grew up in western Kansas. He attended Hoxie High School where he played and lettered in football, basketball, and golf. After completing high school, Ron attended Kansas State University, graduating in 1958 with a bachelor's degree in horticulture.

In 1955, Ron met, and married Sarah Lee Thompson in Indianapolis, Indiana, while attending the Army's Adjutant General Basic Course. Upon graduation, Ron was commissioned as a second lieutenant in the U.S. Army's Adjutant General's Corps and served on active duty for twenty-two years.

Ron retired from the Army as a Lieutenant Colonel in 1988. During his military career, he earned several meritorious service awards including the Bronze Star Medal, the Army Meritorious Service Medal, and the Army Commendation Medal.

After his military retirement, Ron and Sarah Lee moved to San Marcos, Texas, so Ron could start a second career as an investment advisor with Wells Fargo. This past summer Ron and Sarah Lee celebrated 58 years of marriage.

A guiding principle in Ron's life was to give back to the community. He believed that a person should not only be aware of community issues but should also become actively involved to make a difference. In the early 1980s, Ron was a founding organizer of the Hays County Republican Party, to which he dedicated invaluable time and effort over the years.

The environment and the beautification of San Marcos were Ron's primary interests. Besides being involved in planting numerous trees in public areas, the San Marcos River Walk was in large part Ron's idea; and he was instrumental in helping to secure funding for the project.

Ron is survived by his loving wife Sarah Lee, his son William and wife Charlene, his daughter Samantha, her husband Robert Jefferson, and their two children Roper and Remington. Ron's children remember him as a loving and caring father who was very well read and always ready and able to answer the numerous questions they had. Ron is also survived by his sister Veronica and her husband Jack Money, and his brother Timothy.

A celebration of Ron's life will be held Saturday, December 14, from 2:00 to 5:00 p.m. at the family home. Fort Sam Houston will accept Ron's ashes for internment with full military honors in February. Memorial contributions in Ron's name can be made to Gary Job Corps in San Marcos. For additional contribution information, please contact Gary Job Corps directly at 512-555-5871.

Obituary Template

(Deceased's name) died at the age of XX at (home, hospital, nursing home, etc.) in (city and state) on (date) due to (cause of death, if desired).

(Deceased's first name or nickname) was born on (date) in (city and state) to (names of father and mother). (Deceased's name) attended (name of high school) where he/she (was a cheerleader/athlete/played in the band/ was an honor student, etc.) After completing high school, (deceased's name) attended (name of college or university) graduating in (year) with a (type of degree).

After graduation, (Deceased's first name or nickname)........ (*write something about work or career -- see sample obituaries*).

In (year) (deceased's first name or nickname) married (name of spouse, including maiden name for women). The couple had (number of children) children, (name(s) of daughter(s) and (name(s) of son(s), typically listed from oldest to youngest).

(*As appropriate, add any details about the deceased's work/life in the community/military service/etc. See Appendix A and sample obituaries*).

(As appropriate) (Deceased's name) is survived by (names and relationships—mother/father/sons/daughters/sisters/brothers/ grandchildren) of (name(s) of city and state). (Deceased's name) was preceded in death by (name(s) and relationship(s)).

Funeral arrangements are being handled by (name of mortuary or funeral home). (Deceased's name) will be (buried/memorialized—give details) at (location) on (date). (*Add any details concerning flowers or donations—see sample obituaries*).

Note: Consider omitting DOB and city of birth to avoid identity theft.

Appendix J: Veterans Administration Benefits for Survivors

Under certain circumstances, Veterans Administration (VA) benefits are available to the spouse, children, and/or parents of a deceased veteran. Some of these benefits are available only if the veteran had a service-connected disability, and the disability was directly related to the cause of death. A comprehensive guide to VA benefits, "The Federal Benefits for Veterans, Dependents, and Survivors," is available online at www.va.gov.opa/publications/benefits. We strongly encourage the survivors of veterans, especially retirees, to download this guide and read it to see what benefits may be available.

Eligibility for Benefits

Eligibility for most VA benefits is based upon discharge from active military service under other than dishonorable conditions. Active service means full-time service, other than active duty for training, as a member of the Army, Navy, Air Force, Marine Corps, Coast Guard, or as a commissioned officer of the Public Health Service, Environmental Science Services Administration or National Oceanic and Atmospheric Administration, or its predecessor, the Coast and Geodetic Survey.

Dependency and Indemnity Compensation

The survivor of a veteran whose discharge was under conditions other than dishonorable may be eligible for Dependency and Indemnity Compensation (DIC) if one of the following directly caused or contributed to the veteran's death:

- A disease or injury incurred or aggravated in the line of duty while on active duty or active duty for training

- An injury, heart attack, cardiac arrest, or stroke incurred or aggravated in the line of duty while on inactive duty for training

- A service-connected disability or a condition directly related to a service-connected disability

DIC also may be paid to certain survivors of veterans who were totally disabled from service-connected conditions at the time of death, even though their service-connected disabilities did not cause their deaths. The survivor qualifies if the veteran met any one of the following criteria:

- Continuously rated totally disabled for a period of ten years immediately preceding death

- Continuously rated totally disabled from the date of military discharge and for at least five years immediately preceding death

- A former POW who was continuously rated totally disabled for a period of at least one year immediately preceding death

Payments will be offset by any amount received from judicial proceedings brought on by the veteran's death. When the surviving spouse is eligible for payments under the military's Survivor Benefit Plan (SBP), only the amount of SBP greater than DIC is payable. If DIC is greater than SBP, only DIC is payable. The veteran's discharge must have been under conditions other than dishonorable.

Surviving spouses of veterans who died on or after January 1, 1993, receive a basic rate, plus additional payments for dependent children, for the aid and attendance of another person who is a patient in a nursing home or who requires the regular assistance of another person, or if the surviving spouse is permanently housebound.

Assistance with Benefits

State

The Texas Veterans Commission (TVC) is the designated agency of the State of Texas to represent the State and its veterans before the U.S. Department of Veterans Affairs (VA). The Commission is nationally recognized for its expertise in helping veterans get the most benefits to which they are entitled. Similar Commissions exist in most other states. The Commission represents veterans in filing VA disability claims and during VA appeals processes, and assists dependents with survivor benefits. The agency has more than seventy-five claims counselors accredited by the VA to represent veterans with disability claims and appeals. Counselors in more than twenty-five locations in Texas including Austin, Dallas, Houston, San Antonio, and Waco help veterans and their families with questions regarding benefits, survivor and dependent needs, filling out VA paperwork, and medical issues. Information about TVC can be found online at www.tvc.texas.gov

Local

In Texas, every county with a population of 200,000 or more has a Veterans Services Officer whose salary is paid by the county. (Other states have similar programs on the county level, but population requirements vary based on location.) The County Veterans Services Officer does not work for the Veterans Administration (VA), but does coordinate closely with the Texas Veterans Commission. Approximately seventy-five to eighty percent of a Veterans Services Officer's workload is handling veteran's benefits. We recommend that the family of a deceased veteran contact the County Veterans Services Officer as soon as possible after death to obtain information, advice, and assistance regarding benefits eligibility. The office location and telephone number of the County Veterans Services Officer can be found in your local telephone directory or online.

Appendix K: How to Replace Lost Military Separation Documents

If lost or misplaced, military service separation documents (usually referred to as a DD-214) can be obtained from the National Archives in about three to four weeks. You will need the following to apply:

- The veteran's complete name used while in service

- Service number (usually it's the same as the social security number)

- Social security number

- Branch of service

- Dates of service

- Date and place of birth (especially if the service number is not known)

All requests must be signed and dated by the veteran or his/her next of kin. Next of kin of a deceased veteran must provide proof of death of the veteran. A copy of the death certificate, a letter from a funeral home, or a published obituary will suffice.

For service members in the Army before 1960, there's an eighty percent chance their service records were destroyed by a fire where military records are stored. If the service member was in the Air Force before 1964 and his/her name comes after Hubbard, James E., there's a seventy-five percent chance the records were destroyed. If the service member's service records were destroyed, the National Archives will try to provide proof of service based on other types of military records. They will need the following information, so you might as well include it on your first application:

- Place of discharge

- Last unit of assignment

- Place of entry into the service, if known

You can request documents either online or by mail. The paper application, Standard Form 180, can be retrieved by going to:

http://www.archives.gov/veterans/military-service-records/standard-form-180.html

The online application, eVetRecs, will work only with Internet Explorer. Click *Launch the eVetRecs system to start your request Online* and answer the questions. When you are finished, print, sign, and either fax or mail the signature page to the address listed on the request form.

If you do not require an official copy of the DD-214 and the veteran is or was enrolled with the VA Health Care System, you may be able to contact the local VA hospital and ask them for a copy of the DD-214 form.

If time is of the essence, *Aardvark Research Group* is an organization that has provided reliable, short turnaround service to veterans and their families. ARG is located near the National Personnel Records Center in St. Louis. They will provide certified copies of original DD-214's, usually within a day or so; but their services are not free. The cost at the time of this writing is $89. Records can be ordered online through their website: www.aardvarkresearchgroup.com

Appendix L: Important Contacts You May Need

- **Contact information for military retiree services:**

  o **Arlington National Cemetery** (877-907-8585)

  o **U.S. Army**

    ▪ Office of the Deputy Chief of Staff, G-1
      DAPE-HRPD-RSO (Retirement Services Office)
      200 Stovall St.
      Alexandria, VA 22332-0470
      703-325-9158

    ▪ HQDA Casualty Operations Center (*to report a retiree death*)
      800-636-3317

  o **U.S. Air Force**
    AFPC/DPPRT
    550 C Street W, Ste. 3
    Randolph AFB, TX 78150-4713
    210-565-4663

  o **Department of Navy**
    NPC PERS-675R
    Retired Activities Section
    5720 Integrity Drive
    Millington, TN 38055-6640
    866-827-5672

- o **U.S. Marine Corps**
  Headquarters, USMC
  Manpower and Reserve Affairs
  (MMSR-6)
  3280 Russell Road
  Quantico, VA 22134-5103
  800-336-4649 Option #0

- o **U.S. Coast Guard**
  Commanding Officer (RAS)
  U.S. Coast Guard
  Personnel Service Center
  444 SE Quincy St.
  Topeka, KS 66683-3591
  800-772-8724

- **Defense Finance and Accounting Service (DFAS)**
  U.S. Military Retirement Pay
  Post Office Box 7130
  London, KY 40742-7130
  800-321-1080 or 216-522-5955/800-269-5170 (for deceased members)

  My pay website: https://mypay.dfas.mil/mypay.aspx

  Retiree/annuitant website: http://www.dfas.mil/retiredmilitary.html

  For settlement of military retired pay and to start the application process for survivor annuity benefits such as RSFPP, SBP, RCSBP and SSBP, visit the website: (www.dfas.mil)

- **Medicare:** 800-633-4227; www.medicare.gov

- **Military ID Card Facilities:** 800-538-9552

- **Military OneSource:** 800-342-9647

For military and family support services. Military One Source can provide information and links to the American Red Cross and other military emergency resources.

Web site: (www.militaryonesource.com)

- **Military Records**: To request a DD-214 military record form, call 866- 272-6272.

Website: (www.archives.gov)

- **Office of Personnel Management:** 888-767-6738

To report the death of a retired civil service employee and check on benefits.

Website: (www.opm.gov)

- **Social Security Administration**: 800-772-1213

To stop social security payments, if any.

Surviving spouses and dependent children may also be eligible for death and/or survivor benefits. Website: (www.ssa.gov)

- **Social Security Benefits Estimator**: 800-772-1213 or 800-325-0778 for the deaf

- **TRICARE** for Life: 866-773-0404

- **USAA Survivor Relations Team** (for USAA members only): 800-531-1045

- **Veterans Affairs (VA) Information**

   o **Department of Veterans Affairs**: 800-827-1000. For settlement of veteran insurance programs such as SGLI, VGLI, NSLI, USGLI or DIC and to ask about benefits for the surviving spouse and eligible children, visit the website: (www.va.gov)

   o **VA Regional Office Locator**: 800-827-1000

   o **Benefits and Services**: 800-827-1000

o **Burial and Memorial Benefits**: www.cem.va.gov/

o **Graves Information**: 877-907-8199; www.benefits. va.gov.benefits/

Appendix M: Checklists for Pre-Planning, Survivors and Executors

	Pre-planning Checklist	
	Pre-planning Actions	Date
	Collect and document vital information. (See Appendix A)	
	Evaluate your life insurance. Do you have SBP as a military retiree?	
	Consult with your financial advisor and/or accountant.	
	Consult with an attorney regarding a will, trusts, and powers of attorney.	
	Designate a primary and alternate executor for your estate.	
	Prepare a will if you do not have one and have it properly executed.	
	Prepare advance directives, including a DNR order and both durable and medical POAs.	
	Evaluate hospice care.	
	Designate a funeral home/mortuary to handle your death services.	
	Document your wishes for funeral and burial services.	
	Consider pre-paid funeral and burial services or else arrange for funds to be available to survivors to cover these immediate expenses.	
	Survivors' Checklist **(Steps to take following the death of a loved one)**	
	If the deceased's death was unattended:	
	Call hospice if applicable or 911 if the deceased was not under hospice care.	
	Locate and have available for EMS the DNR document, if it exists.	
	Notify the deceased's doctor.	
	Obtain a legal pronouncement of death.	

Contact Checklist for Family or Executor	
Life insurance agent or company; report death and request claim instructions/forms.	
Medical and health insurance companies, including Medicare/Medicaid (as appropriate)	
Banks, credit unions, and savings and loan companies.	
Landline/cell phone, cable and Internet services, as appropriate.	
Utility companies to change or stop service.	
Post office to stop or forward mail if applicable.	
Contact Experian, Equifax, and TransUnion; in addition, mail copies of death certificate to them.	
Mail copies of the death certificate to appropriate banks, credit unions, savings and loan companies, and other financial institutions. Include a written request that the deceased's accounts be closed or changed to joint ownership.	
Report the death to the SSA, IRS and DMV.	
Starting 30 days after death through at least 90 days, periodically check deceased's credit reports for suspicious activity.	
Stop any automated payments from bank accounts.	
Cancel club/gym memberships if needed.	
Check banks and insurance companies for accidental death policies, if applicable.	

Contact an undertaker to arrange for transportation of the body.	
Notify close family and friends.	
Report the death of a military retiree to the DFAS Casualty Office at 800-321-1080.	
Locate keys and open safe deposit box to access any pertinent documents.	
If a veteran, notify the VA. Inquire about survivor benefits.	
Notify trade union, fraternal or religious organizations to inquire about burial benefits associated with membership and any participation in the funeral/burial services.	
Notify social security (this should be done automatically by TRS).	
As appropriate, arrange for the care of dependent children or parents.	
As applicable, notify the deceased's employer.	
If the deceased lived alone:	
Arrange for security of the residence and all contents.	
As appropriate, arrange for the care of pets.	
Arrange for care or disposal of any houseplants.	
Inspect the refrigerator and arrange for the disposal of any perishables.	
Notify the post office to hold mail until claimed by the executor of the will.	
Arrange to stop newspaper deliveries.	
If the deceased lived in a rental, contact landlord to arrange lease termination.	
Review decedent's wishes regarding death services and burial/cremation.	
Make arrangements with the funeral home for death services and burial.	
Write an obituary and arrange for publication.	
Schedule and complete funeral and burial services.	
Purchase 10 to 20 copies of the certified death certificate.	
Locate the will. (Check the safety deposit box.)	
Determine who is authorized to access the safety deposit box and keys.	
Notify the deceased's attorney and/or executor of the deceased's estate.	
Request employer information about benefits, insurance, and pay due.	

Checklist for Executor of the Estate	
Gather important documents listed below (and in Appendix A). (May be in safety deposit box.)	
Death certificate	
Will	
Social Security Card	
Birth Certificates for deceased, spouse and children	
Marriage certificate	
Military discharge papers/DD-214 if applicable	
Divorce decrees if applicable	
Life insurance policies	
Home and auto insurance policies	
Titles to motor vehicles	
Deeds to all real estate	
Lease or rental contracts	
Medical insurance cards and policies	
Retirement benefits documentation	
Bank statements	
Brokerage account documentation	
Securities and investments (stocks and bonds) documentation	
Documents related to any businesses owned	
Most recent local, state, and federal tax returns	
Meet with the deceased's CPA concerning tax issues.	
If appropriate, retain an attorney to assist with estate matters.	
File for probate.	
Probate the will.	
Administer the estate of the deceased.	
Close the estate and distribute the assets.	

GLOSSARY OF TERMS

Advance Directive: A legal document in which the signer gives directions or designates another person to make health care decisions for the signer if the signer becomes incapable of making such decisions.

Affidavit: A written declaration made under oath before a notary public or other authorized officer.

Deceased: No longer living; dead.

Decedent: A dead person.

Declarant: A person who has executed (signed in the presence of witnesses) a do-not-resuscitate order, or on whose behalf a do-not-resuscitate order has been executed pursuant to applicable laws.

Demise: The end of existence or activity. Death.

Estate: The sum of an individual's assets; a person's net worth at any point in time, alive or dead.

Execute a Will: To cause a will to be legally valid by signing it in the presence of witnesses.

Holographic Will: A Last Will and Testament that is written in the testator's own handwriting.

Intestate: Dying without a will.

Medical Power of Attorney: Also known as a Health Care Power of Attorney. A Medical Power of Attorney gives someone you trust the legal authority to act on your behalf regarding health care decisions if you ever become incapacitated or unable to communicate.

Nuncupative Will: An oral last will and testament that is spoken out loud.

Out-of-Hospital Do-Not-Resuscitate Order: A document directing that no resuscitation be initiated for a person whose respiration and circulation has ceased if that person is in a setting outside of a hospital, nursing home, or mental health facility.

Power of Attorney: A written document granting a trusted person (the agent) the legal authority to act on behalf of another person (the principal) in certain specified matters such as financial dealings, medical matters, or in general.

Probate: Probate is the term that describes the legal process of transferring property from the "estate" of a deceased person to the parties named in his or her will. Probate is a court-supervised process that authenticates a decedent's last will and testament (if there is one); locates and determines the value of the decedent's assets; pays the decedent's final bills, estate taxes and/or inheritance taxes (if any); and distributes to the decedent's rightful heirs what (if anything) is left.

Self-Proved Will: A type of will that is validated by attaching or including an affidavit which is signed by the witnesses to the will in front of an officer authorized to administer oaths, such as a notary public. The purpose of the "self-proving affidavit" is to confirm that the witnesses actually saw the testator sign the will and to alleviate the need to obtain affidavits from the witnesses after the testator dies.

Testator: Any person who makes a will. A person who has written and executed a last will and testament that is in effect at the time of his/her death.

Life comes with an expiration date; sometimes sooner than expected. This became true for my dear friend, business partner, and co-author, Tommye White, who passed away on June 14, 2016. The biography in this book does not do justice to Tommye. She was a West Texas woman who was fun, kind, intelligent, and self-reliant. Tougher than boot leather when she had to be, Tommye was the most caring, generous, sweetest, and sometimes the most stubborn woman I ever knew. Her contributions to the writing of this book are immeasurable.

Rest in Peace, Tommye.
You will forever be missed.